Trustable and Preshus Friends

*I like to write letters but I
like to get the ansers still better.*

Your little frend   Elsie Leslie

Foreword by
Julie Harris

Edited by
Jane Douglass

Harcourt   Brace   Jovanovich   New York and London

4

Grateful acknowledgment is made to Frankin D. Roosevelt, Jr.,
literary executor for Eleanor Roosevelt, for permission
to reprint the letters of Elliott Roosevelt;
and to the American Foundation for the Blind for permission
to reprint the letters of Helen Keller.

Printed in the United States of America

Library of Congress Cataloging in Publication Data
Main entry under title:
Trustable and preshus friends.
1. Lyde, Elsie Leslie, 1881-1966. 2. Actors—United
States—Biography. I. Douglass, Jane.
PN2287.L94T7   791.43′028′0924 [B]   77-73048
ISBN 0-15-191318-8

First edition

BCDE

5

_To_ _E_lsie and _E_dwin
with love

Foreword

This is an enchanted book about an enchanted child of the theatre. It took me back to the days of Gentlemen and Ladies—a gentle time—a time of love. Elsie Leslie was Everyone's Heart's Darling—especially the darling of three famous, fascinating men: Mark Twain, Joseph Jefferson, and William Gillette, whom she called Leo. Any child who dreams about the theatre will love this book and fall in love with Elsie. Oh, those eyes of hers! They remind me of the wonder and mystery I glimpse in the eyes of another famous American actress, Maude Adams. And maybe that look accounts for Elsie and Maude bewitching so many rapt audiences and becoming a legend in their time.

I wish I had known Elsie Leslie when she played Little Lord Fauntleroy and her Prince and the Pauper and even Lydia Languish—her last play before her retirement at eighteen. But I was fortunate to meet her in the last years of her life when she was Mrs. Edwin Milliken. I was going to be in a production of William Wycherley's *The Country Wife* with Lawrence Harvey and Pamela Brown, produced by Daniel Blum. Elsie wrote me a letter asking if I would like to wear the dress she was supposed to wear when she almost played Margery Pinchwife in Wycherley's classic Restoration comedy. (It had been worn by Ada Rehan when she played the part.)

I called Elsie at her hotel on Manhattan's East Side and we arranged to meet. When I came to the Millikens' apartment, I was greeted by a lovely, charming lady, with those sweet, mysterious eyes, and a darling man—small and bird-like, Elsie's husband, Edwin Milliken. We had a good visit and were drawn to each other right away. Elsie showed me the Pinchwife dress but I explained that the costumes for our production had been designed in England for George Devine's production at the Royal Court and were coming from London to be used by us. Then we talked and she told me of her friendship with Hal Holbrook, who she had seen as her old friend Mark Twain in Hal's one-man play *Mark Twain Tonight!* and when she saw Hal on stage it was like seeing her dear friend after all those years come back to life. Elsie asked me about myself and my family, my son, Peter, who was then six or seven. One of the things that Elsie said has always stayed with me. She said, "An audience always demands so much from you." I have always thought of that eight-year-old child touring America from coast to coast and finally being able to sit still at Road's End, the country retreat in Vermont, bought with her earnings.

Of the many treats in store for the reader of this darling book, the greatest is Mark Twain's letter to Elsie, explaining the slipper he embroidered for her—the mate having been made by Mr. Gillette. Mark Twain's inspired madcap humor is memorable. And then there are the pictures! Some will make you gasp with joy at the wonder and beauty of this remarkable child. We should all have a trustable and precious friend like little Elsie Leslie in our lives. And the supporting cast in her life story is exciting—Eleanor Roosevelt; Helen Keller; the great English actor Sir Henry Irving; and Oliver Wendell Holmes, who discourages Elsie from being a writer. There is a quaintness and beauty in this book that is hard to find in our lives today. Hurrah for children!

Julie Harris

New York
1977

Prologue

Long before little Mary Pickford delighted an astonished public by washing her hair in front of a camera, or Freddie Bartholomew came to Hollywood to play Copperfield, or Shirley Temple danced with Bojangles, or Jackie Coogan's wistful face proved the perfect companion to Charlie Chaplin's Tramp, another child had walked into the hearts of theatrical audiences—a real child this time, in a real theatre, where plays really happen. Her name was Elsie Leslie and she was America's first child star. Ninety years later, The New York Public Library has a permanent exhibition about her career in its Library and Museum of the Performing Arts at Lincoln Center. It is enjoyed by people of all ages. Children speak of it as "Elsie's Doll House" as, indeed, its charming arrangement suggests.

The letters included in this book—those written to Elsie Leslie as a child and her replies—reveal that she knew not only great theatrical personages of her time but other famous people as well. She was a favorite of Sir Henry Irving, Edwin Booth, E. H. Sothern, Joseph Jefferson, William Gillette, and William Faversham; of the producers Daniel Frohman and David Belasco—all of whom loved her as a fascinating child and a gifted artist. Among her literary friends were Oliver Wendell Holmes, Mark Twain, Laurence Hutton, and W. H. Patten; Mary Mapes Dodge, Frances Hodgson Burnett, and Kate Douglas Wiggin. Artists included the famous painter, William Merritt Chase; the illustrators Reginald Birch, Frederick S. Church, Edward B. Edwards, and F. Schuyler Mathews. She knew Phillips Brooks, the best loved of all Episcopal ministers; the wonder child, Helen Keller; and little Eleanor Roosevelt.

Elsie Leslie did not come from a theatrical background. Her father, Benjamin Tanner Lyde, was a successful merchant in Newark, New Jersey; her mother, while American born, was of English descent—a cousin of Angela Burdette Coutts, the British philanthropist and friend of Charles Dickens. In the English manner Elsie always addressed her parents as Mama and Papa. When her father's health failed and he lost his business, Joseph Jefferson, then living in nearby Hohokus, befriended the family by taking Elsie and her sister Dora into his theatrical company. He was then preparing a production of *Rip Van Winkle*. After seeing Elsie and Dora in rehearsal, Mr. Jefferson said to Mrs. Lyde, "Dora is the beauty but it is the little one who has the brains. It is she who will make the actress." Dora was then fifteen and Elsie just four and a half—quite right to play Little Meenie. The Lyde relatives were strict Methodists who disapproved of the theatre. When the financial situation made it necessary for the children to continue working, it was decided that Elsie and Dora should use their middle name of Leslie on the stage.

When the engagement in *Rip Van Winkle* ended, Elsie and Dora, at Mr. Jefferson's suggestion, called upon Daniel Frohman at the Lyceum Theatre. Mr. Frohman had recently acquired this beautiful little theatre on Fourth Avenue and Twenty-third Street in New York City. His first production there was *The Highest Bidder*, hitherto an unknown comedy which E. H. Sothern had brought to the manager's attention. This play was a great hit and made a star of Mr. Sothern. Dora Leslie knew this and had heard that Mr. Frohman was casting another play for the actor in which she greatly wanted a part. Alas—Mr. Frohman said the cast for the new piece, *The Great Pink Pearl*, was complete and there was no part for Miss Dora. However, as this play was fairly short, he planned to present a curtain raiser with it and had in mind a one-act play by his friend, Gus Thomas, in which there was a little girl. Mr. Frohman had seen the girls with Mr. Jefferson in *Rip Van Winkle*. Mr. Frohman wondered if Miss Elsie would like to act with Mr. Sothern. Thus began Elsie Leslie's happy association with Daniel Frohman and E. H. Sothern. The curtain raiser proved to be *Editha's Burglar*, dramatized by Augustus Thomas from Mrs. Burnett's story of that name. Hardly more than a dialogue, almost a tear-jerker, the playlet was enormously successful. It told of a criminal who is rebuffed and redeemed by an innocent child. There were only three characters. Elsie Leslie was Editha; Herbert Archer played her father; and E. H. Sothern made a great thing of the role of the burglar. Mr. Frohman was so delighted with Elsie's performance, he made her a member of his Lyceum Company. Her birthday falling in August of that year (1887), she was just six years old.

The most interesting review of *Editha's Burglar* is that by Professor George C. Odell in his monumental *Annals of the Stage,* Volume VIII:

The Lyceum having closed on July 16th, re-opened with the same attraction, *The Highest Bidder* with Sothern, Lemoyne, Piggott, Archer and Belle Archer in their former roles, but with Fanny Addison and Kitty Wilson replacing Alice Crowley and Vida Crowther. The run terminated on Monday, September 19th. On the twentieth, Frohman produced *The Great Pink Pearl* by R. C. Carton and Cecil Raleigh (the latter directing), casting it extremely well with members of the Sothern company and the new aggregation which was, within a short time, to establish itself as a permanent stock company of the house. . . . *Editha's Burglar* was given the same night, with Sothern and Archer, and that clever child, Elsie Leslie, beginning with it her remarkable career. For certain Wednesday matinees, we were enlivened with *The Highest Bidder* and *Editha's Burglar.*

When Mr. Frohman decided to send *The Great Pink Pearl* on tour, he secured William Gillette to take over the leading role. Mrs. Lyde was glad to find that *Editha's Burglar* was also to tour, and thus it was that Mama brought about Elsie's life-long friendship with William Gillette. The Gillettes had no children and during the Boston run of *Editha's Burglar* they became devoted to the charming little girl. Mr. Gillette made a great name in both *The*

Great Pink Pearl and *Editha's Burglar,* and later he wrote from the Editha play a three act drama which he called *The Burglar*—this time the emphasis was on the burglar rather than upon Editha. Gillette made money with *The Burglar,* for it toured for well over ten years. It also brought about William Gillette's long and profitable association with Maurice Barrymore.

However, for the New York engagement of *The Burglar,* Mr. Gillette had to be content with another Editha because, by this time, he had secured the Fauntleroy part for Elsie Leslie in the anticipated dramatization by Frances Hodgson Burnett of her famous story *Little Lord Fauntleroy*. This first American production of the play was by the Boston Museum Stock Company on September 10th, 1888. This was an eventful year for both the author and for Elsie Leslie. The Boston Museum production of *Little Lord Fauntleroy* was so successful that the play was soon purchased by the New York firm of Sanger and French. T. Henry French proposed to open his new Broadway Theatre with it.

Before the play could be brought to New York, Mr. French was informed that a committee of prominent Bostonians had written to The New York Society for the Prevention of Cruelty to Children in behalf of the little star. Elsie Leslie had become so loved in Boston her admirers feared that she was being overworked and her education neglected. It is unknown who headed this committee, but there is evidence of its far reaching effect upon Elsie's case and that of other children working in the entertainment field. The moving spirit and legal counsel for The Society was Mr. Elbridge T. Gerry. He became interested in Elsie's case and when he knew her well, he became very fond of her and interested in the family. Their friendship lasted until his death, and Elsie's parents were so appreciative of Mr. Gerry's efforts they continued to warmly support the work he had done.

The influence of this organization is felt today. Before

a child can act professionally in this country, he.or she must be seven years of age, and the parents or guardians must secure a permit from the Mayor of the town where the child lives. In New York, The Society and the Actor's Equity Association work together to see that stage children are given proper protection.

It has been a long, educative process and the dedication of Mr. Elbridge T. Gerry, child-lover and philanthropist, has long been valued. It was he who wrote the law protecting the stage child; it was he who put it through the Legislature of New York. Of course, certain individuals fought him, sneering at The Society for the Prevention of Cruelty to Children, calling it The Gerry Society. It was a long struggle, for it was not until 1911 that the law which gave to the stage child the same protection given children working in factories and mills was passed. Fortunately, Elsie Leslie was seven years old at the time of the New York production of *Little Lord Fauntleroy*.

Little Lord Fauntleroy as a play made further history in 1888 when it was instrumental in securing an amendment to the copyright law. A plagiarized version based upon the book, then at the height of its fame, was produced in London at The Prince of Wales Theatre by an unscrupulous man by the name of Seebohm. Mrs. Burnett was in Italy at the time. When she learned about this, she rushed to London with her own dramatization in her handbag. In London she engaged a lawyer and secured the backing of a group of prominent authors. Guided by an expert barrister, the matter was taken to court and Mrs. Burnett succeeded in having the Seebohm play withdrawn. On May 14, 1888, her own version of the story under the title *The Real Little Lord Fauntleroy* was produced in London at Terry's Theatre. She had a superb cast. Alfred Bishop was the Earl; Brandon Thomas the Barrister; and Vera Berringer, the child used by the despicable Seebohm, was Fauntleroy. The role of the mother, "Dearest," so beautifully played in Boston by Viola Allen, was in London, played by the en-chanting Winifred Emery. *The Real Little Lord Fauntleroy* was a stunning success. A week after the opening it was praised by no less a critic than William Archer in *The London World*. Even then, Mr. Archer was no mean authority on the drama. Many years later, he wrote *The Green Goddess,* the play made famous on stage and screen by George Arliss.

The Real Little Lord Fauntleroy was a remarkable achievement for Frances Hodgson Burnett. The resulting publicity attracted the sympathy of a wide audience and won the support of the British courts. This example of piracy became the test case which resulted in the amendment to the copyright law whereby authors were granted, in perpetuity, dramatic rights to their published works.

In New York in 1888, Daniel Frohman, as well as others, was gratified by the amendment. At the time, he was considering a production of Mark Twain's book *The Prince and the Pauper,* and he hoped to do this while the popularity of the story, as well as the interest in the child actress, was high. In his book, *Memories of a Manager,* Mr. Frohman has told of his difficulties with Mark Twain in connection with this production of *The Prince and the Pauper.* Of one thing Mr. Frohman was sure, from the start. Mark Twain's sole condition was that Elsie Leslie should play both parts.

It was the little actress herself who persuaded her trustable Mr. Clemens that she could, indeed, play both prince and pauper. Elsie never addressed Samuel Clemens as Mark Twain; such familiarity would have been unthinkable in those days. Recalling her experience, Elsie later said:

"At first Mr. Clemens was so astounded at my suggestion, he could not speak at all. Then he thundered at me:

"Impossible! Impossible!! You are not twins, Elsie, and where under the sun could another child be found?"

"But I want to play both parts," said I.

"My God, child, it will be longer than Hamlet."

"That's all right, Sir. I can learn it."

As incredible as it must seem, thus was the matter settled. When Mark Twain insisted that Elsie Leslie play both parts in the original production of 1890, his love for her was balanced by his confidence in her genius. Once negotiations were completed, he was glad to leave matters to Daniel Frohman, then a leading producer in New York. The choice of the dramatist for *The Prince and the Pauper* was Abby Sage Richardson. Mr. Frohman had known her from earlier days at *The Tribune;* she had done translations and adaptations for him and was also popular as a lecturer upon historical and literary subjects. Furthermore, Mark Twain also knew and admired Mrs. Richardson, the widow of Albert Dean Richardson, so he was pleased that she was to make a play of his book. He was also satisfied with the choice of David Belasco as the director. David Belasco's contribution to the American Theatre is now too well known to discuss here. What is of interest is this example of his early work as a director with experienced actors and his rare understanding of the theatrical child.

When William Faversham was preparing his revival of *The Prince and the Pauper,* he was indebted to this early production. Mrs. Richardson's play was used as the basis of the dramatization by Amelie Rivers who sought to strengthen the Miles Hendon role. Needless to say, it would be played by William Faversham, who had toured in the play with Elsie Leslie so long before. The part of Miles Hendon was a favorite with the actor who, apparently, played it to the hilt. Mr. Faversham was highly praised, also, for the beauty and taste with which he produced *The Prince and the Pauper* at the Booth Theatre in November, 1920. In this elaborate production, the role of the young Princess Elizabeth was played by the late Claire Eames, then making her theatrical debut. Ruth Finlay, an attractive young actress, was entrusted with the dual role. From the producer's view, it is cheaper to follow this precedent. So far as known there are only two performances of the play when two persons were used. The first was when Mrs.

Clemens prepared a performance as a surprise for her husband at Christmas, when Susy, their eldest daughter, played the prince and Margaret Warner, the niece of William Gillette, was the pauper. In the second instance, in the film when Errol Flynn played Miles Hendon in 1936, the Mauch twins were found to play both boys.

Records show that the original production of *The Prince and The Pauper* made a great deal of money. It earned more, perhaps, for its author and producer than for the little actress whose dream it was. One likes to recall Mark Twain's curtain speech the night of the opening at the Broadway Theatre in New York on January 20th, 1890. With Elsie's hand in his he said: "I have always felt there was a rattling good play in *The Prince and the Pauper*. I tried it myself about fifteen years ago and found I was no playwright. So Mrs. Richardson has done it for me, and I realize now that . . . I have had in my mind's eye just such an idyll as we have seen this evening. It is indeed the realization of a dream."

The following morning the critic of the *New York Herald* wrote: "They made a pretty picture the two of them at that moment—the world-worn humorist and the baby actress." In those days there were no photographers to take flash pictures of even so important an opening as this. However, the *New York Herald* sent its staff artist, Henry Pruett Share, to make a sketch of Mark Twain and Elsie Leslie as they stood there before the curtain. It is sad that a diligent search fails to locate the original drawing which may have perished by this time. This is regrettable because it is the only known picture of Elsie Leslie with Mark Twain.

There have been other children who have won distinction in American Theatre, but none of the stature of Elsie Leslie. Before she was eight she had carried the burden of a play written around the character of a child. No other child had done anything like this, earning at such tender years, the position of star and the salary of an adult. No other child convinced a successful author that she could give longer life to one of his books by acting in it in New York and across the country. Before she was twelve Elsie Leslie had played two seasons with Joseph Jefferson, one with E. H. Sothern, and another with William Gillette. Her favorite play was *The Prince and the Pauper*. She never tired of it and it supported Elsie and her family for three and a half years.

An early marriage to Jefferson Winter, a son of William Winter the drama critic, which ended in divorce, took Elsie Leslie away from the theatre for a dozen years. In 1912 she returned briefly to star with George Arliss in Louis N. Parker's play, *Disraeli,* in New York and Chicago. In an unselfish effort to save the marriage, she did not tour with *Disraeli,* the play in which George Arliss made one of his greatest hits in the theatre. In 1918 Elsie Leslie was married to the late Mr. Edwin J. Milliken, a successful Canadian-American businessman. When Mr. Milliken asked her what she wanted most to do, Elsie said she wanted to travel. His reply was, "Well—I should think you would have had your fill of that."

"It would seem so," said Elsie, "for I have been almost everywhere. But I never saw much of the world. I had to sleep during the day because I had to work at night."

So travel they did, eventually returning to live in New York until her death in 1966.

When *The Prince and the Pauper* was produced in New York in 1890, Elsie Leslie received as many floral tributes as does an opera star of 1977. She appreciated them all just as she loved all sorts of messages from many people young and old. However, no gift meant as much to her as the one from Mark Twain. Charmingly framed, he sent his photograph under which he had written:

ODE.
To Elsie Leslie.

I'll be your friend, your thrall, your knave,
  I'll be your elder brother,
I'll be for love your very slave,
  or anything you'd druther.

Mark.

Jane Douglass
New York 1977

Acknowledgements

To Elsie Leslie, who gave me the pictures and letters and entrusted me with these memories. She did not give me these treasures because she thought I would write a book about her. That was my idea, and it was Mr. Milliken's wish that I should guard these mementoes and someday place them where they would be most useful.

In writing this story of the professional life of a little girl, I am grateful for the encouragement and help of the curators of the following collections:

The Boston Atheneum
The Boston Public Library
The Theatre Collection at Harvard
The Mark Twain Memorial in Hartford
The Museum of The City of New York
The New York Society Library
The New York Public Library
The Theatre Collection at Lincoln Center
The Pierpont Morgan Library
The Players

Cast of Characters

Elsie Leslie Lyde (1881–1966)
As Elsie Leslie she was America's first child star.

Dora Lyde (1866–1927)
Elsie's sister. She left the stage in 1896 upon her marriage
to C. V. Fornes.

Evelyn Burdick Lyde (1848–1905)
Benjamin Tanner Lyde (1840–1911)
Elsie's parents.

E. H. Sothern (1859–1933)
American actor and great Shakespearean star.

Daniel Frohman (1851–1940)
leading theatrical producer and president of the Lyceum
Theatre Company.

William Gillette (1855–1937)
American actor and playwright, most often remembered
for his portrayal of Sherlock Holmes and Mr. Dearth
in Barrie's masterpiece, *Dear Brutus*.

Mrs. William Gillette (1860–1888)

Eban Jordan (1851–1916)
Boston merchant, philanthropist, and art patron.

Edna Hall (1835–1896)
Mrs. Davis Culver Hall. As Edna Amelie Brown,
she was a successful concert singer. When Elsie knew her,
Madame Hall was a well-known teacher of voice and a
Boston hostess.

Frances Hodgson Burnett (1849–1924)
juvenile author, remembered best for *Little Lord Fauntleroy,
Sara Crew,* and *The Secret Garden.*

Mildred Aldrich (1852–1928)
Boston newspaper woman, author of *A Hilltop on the Marne.*
She was honored by the French Government for war work
during the First World War, 1914–1918.

Viola Allen (1869–1948)
famous American actress and friend of Elsie Leslie.

W. H. Patten (1868–1936)
illustrator, art editor of Harper & Bros., Publishers.

T. Henry French (1848–1902)
theatrical producer. In association with Frank Sanger
he built the Broadway Theatre. Now demolished, it stood
at Broadway and 41st Street.

Frank Sanger (1849–1904)
actor of more than average ability,
who found his true vocation in theatrical management.

William Merritt Chase (1849–1916)
famous American painter.

Reginald Birch (1856–1943)
artist, noted for his children's book illustrations.

Edward B. Edwards (1873–1948)
this graphic artist designed and gave Elsie Leslie her book-plate.
The quotation on it, *"We that live to please must please to live,"*
is from the prologue written by Samuel Johnson for delivery
by David Garrick when Garrick assumed the management
of the Drury Lane Theatre in London in 1747. Mr. Garrick,
a student of Samuel Johnson, the "Great Cham of Literature,"
is regarded as one of the greatest actors in the history
of the English stage.

Frederick Stuart Church (1842–1924)
illustrator and artist.

Edwin Booth (1833–1895)
one of America's greatest tragedians noted for his Hamlet,
and founder of The Players Club.

Joseph Jefferson (1829–1905)
dearly loved actor and great comedian.

Tommy Russell (1880–1926)
younger brother of Annie Russell, the actress.
As an adult he left the stage
and became a successful art dealer.

Napoleon Sarony (1821–1896)
famous theatrical photographer of the period, known for
his innovative treatment of lighting and pose
to effect a grace and ease in his subjects.

Abby Morton Diaz (1821–1904)
author of a famous doll story, *Polly Cologne.*
Mrs. Diaz is remembered today as one of the founders
of the Woman's Industrial Union in Boston.

Mary Mapes Dodge (1831–1905)
editor of *St. Nicholas,* beloved children's periodical,
and author of *Hans Brinker* or *The Silver Skates.*

Kate Douglas Wiggin (1856–1923)
American educator and author, remembered today
as the creator of *Rebecca of Sunny Brook Farm*
and *The Birds' Christmas Carol.*

S. L. Clemens (1835–1910)
"Mark Twain."

Olivia Langdon Clemens (1845–1904)
Mrs. S. L. Clemens.

Elbridge T. Gerry (1837–1927)
distinguished lawyer and philanthropist who fought
for the protection of children.

Elliott Roosevelt (1860–1894)
brother of President Theodore Roosevelt
and father of Eleanor (1844–1966), who became the wife
of President Franklin D. Roosevelt.

L. C. Prang (1823–1909)
famous Boston lithographer.

F. Schuyler Mathews (1854–1938)
author and illustrator, long associated
with the firm L. C. Prang Co. Mr. Mathews was also
a prominent member of the New England Botanical Society.

David Belasco (1853–1931)
American playwright and producer.

Edward C. Freiberger (1859–1917)
Chicago newspaper man and litterateur.

Helen Keller (1889–1968)

Phillips Brooks (1835–1893)
rector of Trinity Church in Boston; later Bishop
of Massachusetts. He wrote "O Little Town of Bethlehem."

Elizabeth Ely (1858–1941)
headmistress of the Ely School, famous preparatory school
for girls in New York City.

Chauncy Depew (1854–1929)
lawyer, United States Senator, railroad magnate.

Horatio Alger (1832–1899)
clergyman and author of more than 100 enormously popular
books for boys, written to the rags-to-riches formula.
Ragged Dick, Luck and Pluck, and *Tattered Tom*
were his most famous.

Oliver Wendell Holmes (1809–1894)
physician, American man of letters, and father of
the distinguished jurist Oliver Wendell Holmes (1841–1935).

Sir Henry Irving (1838–1905)
British actor, and the first actor to be buried
in Westminster Abbey. *Merchant of Venice* and *The Bells*
were in the repertory of the London Lyceum Theatre Company
when Sir Henry Irving toured America.

Dame Ellen Terry (1847–1926)
Irving's leading lady at the Lyceum and most popular
of all British actresses.

Laurence Hutton (1843–1904)
American essayist, critic, and literary editor
of *Harper's Magazine.*

William Faversham (1868–1940)
third distinguished actor to play Miles Hendon
in *The Prince and the Pauper.*

Otis Skinner (1858–1942)
American actor, star of *Kismut.*
Mr. Skinner was Jack Absolute in Jefferson's production
of *The Rivals* in 1898.

There are literal-minded souls who make good resolutions only on New Year's Day and dutifully begin on January First to keep a diary in a stout volume which they have procured themselves. This was not the way of it with little Elsie Leslie. Papa thought it appropriate for her to own a diary in which he wished her to write down, while they were fresh in her mind, her impressions of plays and players that so fascinated her. He thought this good training in diction, composition, penmanship and orthography. These were long words for a little girl, but Papa explained what they meant, and because she loved him very much, she tried to obey and do what he wished. And so the story of Elsie Leslie, while largely told in letters, really begins with the first entry in the diary from Papa which he gave her at the time of her New York debut in Editha's Burglar *in 1887.*

September 21, 1887

$\mathcal{D}$ear $\mathcal{D}$iary,

When I woke this morning I felt something under my pillow and it was YOU. You are a present from Papa. You are verry pretty being a warm brown with gold letters which say ELSIE LESLIE LYDE. After breakfast I gave Papa a kiss and we had a talking. He said if I write in you faithfully you may help me become a writer and if I write my diary like a letter it will be easier. He said I can keep copies between your pages of some of the letters I write. This will help me to remember what I said and also learn to be careful how I say it. I hope too that it will help my spelling which is dreadful. Dear Papa! He was too kind to say anything about that. Well, I WILL try but I think I shall enjoy more putting in the letters I receive. I mean the most preshus ones. I think this is a good idea, dear Diary, becoz I can read them over and over. Also they will not get lost. At least I hope not.

But I must tell you about yesterday. "Editha's Burglar" opened at the Lyceum Theatre last night. It came on first to raise the curtain. It was verry exciting. Before the curtain went up I was scared. But when we began talking to each other, that is, Mr. Archer who is my Papa in the play and Editha, it was fine and I forgot I was frightened. Mama said I did verry well and so did Mr. Archer and Mr. Sothern who is the burglar before I left and the main play "The Great Pink Pearl" came on. I do love them both verry much and that's all except Dora and I had hot cocoa before we went to bed.

The play is about how the burglar comes to love me so verry much that he won't burgle any more. Now, dear Diary, what do you think of this?

The Lyceum Theatre
Fourth Avenue and Twenty-Third Street
New York Treatre Co., Proprietors
Daniel Frohman, Manager

Elsie, dear,

Mr. and Mrs. Fiske enjoyed "Editha's Burglar", and as he is planning his Christmas Number of The Dramatic Mirror, he would like you to write and tell him about burglars. He thinks by this time you may have something interesting to say. If you will do so, and bring it to me before the performance on Saturday I will take it to him. Perhaps he will publish it.

Affectionately,
Daniel Frohman

Mama thinks this is a good thing   she says Mr. Frohman said I must do it soon becoz the Christmas number of the paper is filling up. In case my letter is printed on Christmas Eve I will head it December 24th 1887. Do you think this will do, dear Diary?

Harrison Grey Fiske (1861–1942), leading figure in the American Theatre for more than thirty years, and husband of Minnie Maddern Fiske, famous actress. He owned and edited the New York Dramatic Mirror (formerly The New York Mirror) from 1881 to 1922, making it a leading dramatic periodical.

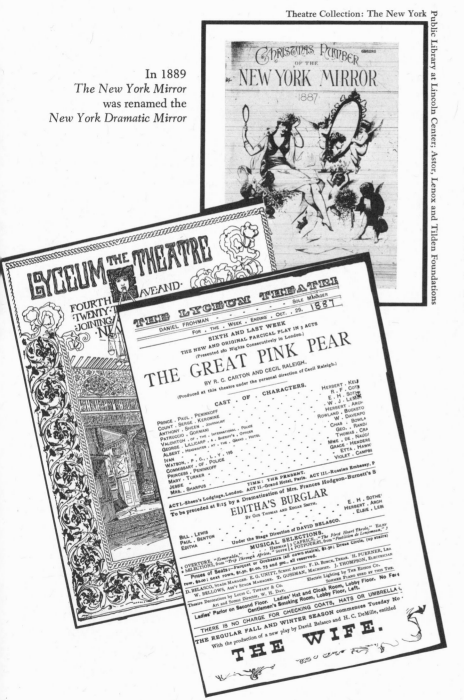

In 1889
The New York Mirror
was renamed the
New York Dramatic Mirror

New York City
December 24th, 1887

Dear Editor,

You want me to write about those wicked persons they call burglars. I know what the newspaper the Sun would say about them. I heard Nurse read to Mary the cook the wicked things they do in burgling and killing people. I think that is awful don't you? Now you want to know what I think of them. Well, I will tell you — if they were all nice burglars like Robin Hood — my sister read me all about him he never used to burgle the poor but always gave them money to buy bread — but he did burgle the rich. Now my burglar Mr. Sothern if they were all as kind to little girls they meet and rap them up in a nice rug to keep them warm when they have a coald and burgle as quietly as he did and not hurt anyone, then leave you with a knife and fork when you ask him, I don't think they are so bad, but then Mr. Sothern was only playing burglar. If he had been a real burglar instead of rapping me up in our rug I think he would have chocked me like the burglar did in Mr. Night's play that I saw the other day — but you know sometimes when my burglar looks so strange and ruff I forget he is Mr. Sothern and think he is a real burglar. Then I get afraid for he seems so real, he looks so ferce at me it makes me kind of shiver but then the curtain goes down and Mr. Sothern kisses me so I know he is not a real burglar but Mr. Sothern for true.

from
Your little friend,
Elsie Leslie

Here I am as Editha. This is when I ask the burglar to be quiet and not frighten my Papa who is writing on his papers in his study.

William Gillette

E. H. Sothern

The Players

Dear Diary,

The dear little Lyceum I think is just the cunningest theatre in the world and I like everyone in the company and I believe they all love me. Now I am both glad and sad becoz Mr. Sothern will not go on tour with "The Great Pink Pearl" and "Editha's Burglar." His part will be taken by Mr. William Gillette. So as sad as I am, I am glad too for I already love Mr. Gillette verry much. He has written the play over. It is longer now but my part is about the same so it is not hard. Mr. Gillette says we open in Boston and the Hollis Street Theatre is VERRY nice. Mrs. Gillette says it gets verry cold in Boston but we shall be allright if we wear long underwear and warm coats. So Mama bought me a new one which I like verry much becoz it has pretty fur trimming. I have a new hat too.

Boston, Mass.
October

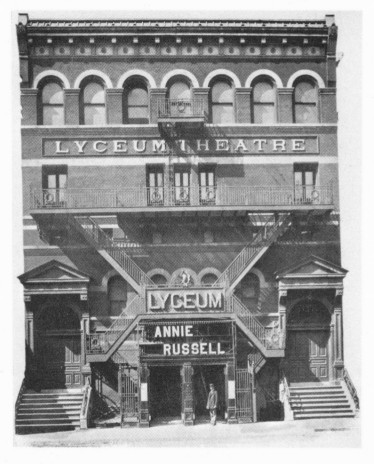

The Hollis Street Theatre IS verry nice but it is large. Mr. Gillette says I am now used to this. He and Mrs. Gillette are very preshus to me now. They have no little girl of their own so it is verry happy for us all. I love my new burglar more all the time but I love Mr. Sothern too and always will. Mr. Gillette reads to me and tells me stories as dear Mr. Jefferson did. Mr. Gillette has told me the story of "She" which is a play made out of a book by a gentleman whose name is Mr. Rider Haggard. Isn't that name odd? "She" is verry thrilling. Once in a while for fun Mr. Gillette and I act it. Dressed in a sheet I am SHE WHO MUST BE OBEYED and he is the hero Leo who is a handsome young man. Mrs. Gillette laughs at us sometimes but I think she likes this becoz it worries her that dear Mr. Gillette works too hard. He says I can call him Leo from now on. Verry often Mrs. Gillette gives us a goodie tea. After it yesterday she gave me a present. It is a beautiful little red velvet case with their pictures inside. Leo is wearing his dashing fur cap and she is looking verry thotful. I shall keep it among my treshurs.

Sir Henry Rider Haggard (1856–1925), English novelist who was, for some years, in government service in South Africa. Among his romantic novels with South African background for which he is best known, are *King Solomon's Mines, Alain Quartermain,* and *She.*

Well — a very unusual thing has happened. "Editha's Burglar" is going to be a book. The Jordan Marsh Company that's a big store in Boston is going to publish it. Leo has sent them photographs of the play and with them in mind Mr. Sandham will make the pictures. Mr. Henry Sandham is an artist who lives in Boston who saw the play and liked it. Mama thinks this is a compliment to me and so does Leo. It will be a small book I think with a pretty cover which children will love and their mothers too. Here is my letter about this.

Dr. Mr. Jordan Marsh and Co.,

   Mama has left it for me to deside if I will let you have my picture for your book I think it wold be very nice. Won't it seem funny to see my verry own picture in Editha like the little girl that used to be in St. Nicholas. I think Mrs. Burnett writes lovely storys   I wrote her a letter and sent it away to paris and told her so and asked her if she wold hurry and write another story just as quick as she could. I am looking for an answer everyday. I like to write letters but I like to get the answers still better. I am going to play Editha in Boston for two weeks and I will ask my mamma to let me come to your store and see all of the butiful things. I used to come every day when I was in Boston last winter.

your little friend
Elsie Leslie
72 West 92 Street
New York City

Henry Sandham (1842–1910), Boston artist and well-known illustrator.

St. Nicholas Magazine, financed by Scribner and The Century, was a popular and successful juvenile periodical. Mary Mapes Dodge was its editor until 1905.

and Mama has given me this one from Mr. Jordan —

Jordan, Marsh & Co.
Importers, Jobbers, & Retailers
Boston
Washington, Summer & Avon Sts.
New York
276 Church Street
Paris
41 Rue de l'Echiqueir
London
9 Red Lion Court

Boston
March 29th, 1888

Dear Mrs. Lyde,

Received your letter of the 20th inst. granting us permission to use the picture of your little girl for the frontispiece of our book, also the letter from little Elsie herself and the two photographic scenes, for which please accept our sincere thanks and find enclosed our check for $25.00 for little Elsie.

Hoping that when you are in this city, you will kindly bring the little girl in to see us.

Very truly yours,
Eben D. Jordan Jr.

Mama has given me this letter to keep and Papa has just put the $25.00 in the Savings Bank for me. He says this is a nest egg so I asked him what that is and he esplaned it. I agreed this is a good idear. And it is the first money I ever made writing something. It is so exciting that I wonder what will happen next. And sure nuff something did. Leo came to tell us that there will be a play about Little Lord Fauntleroy and he has told the lady who wrote it that he thot I would be good in the part! I love this story verry much but of course this will not happen if Mrs. Burnett would rather have a boy. Leo says he doesn't think so but I must not wish for it too hard so I will try not. Leo and I are verry close friends now. He is the most trustable friend I have becoz he never says he will do anything unless he surely does it.

BOSTON MUSEUM

ESTABLISHED 1841

FORTY EIGHTH REGULAR SEASON. MR. R. M. FIELD, MANAGER.

LITTLE · LORD · FAUNTLEROY

DRAMATIZED BY MRS. FRANCES HODGSON-BURNETT

FROM HER OWN CHARMING STORY.

First Production in the United States

· · · COMMENCING · · ·

MONDAY, SEPTEMBER 10, 1888,

· · AND CONTINUING · ·

EVENINGS AT 7.45, AND WEDNESDAY AND
SATURDAY AFTERNOONS AT 2.

☞ ☞ ☞

UNTIL FURTHER NOTICE

☞ ☞ ☞

EARL OF DORINCOURT . . . . Mr. HENRY M. PITT
MR. HAVISHAM, A SOLICITOR . . . . Mr. C. LESLIE ALLEN
SILAS HOBBS, A GROCER . . . . Mr. GEORGE W. WILSON
WILKINS, A GROOM . . . . Mr. JAMES NOLAN
HIGGINS, A FARMER . . . . Mr. THOMAS L. COLEMAN
THOMAS, A VALET . . . . Mr. H. P. WHITTEMORE
JAMES, A FOOTMAN . . . . Mr. HERBERT PATTEE
CEDRIC ERROL, LORD FAUNTLEROY . . . . . . ELSIE LESLIE
DICK TIPTON, A SHOEBLACK . . . . Miss MIRIAM O'LEARY
MRS. ERROL . . . . Miss VIOLA ALLEN
MINNA . . . . Miss ANNIE M. CLARKE
MARY . . . . Miss KATE RYAN
JANE . . . . Miss GRACE ATWELL

ACT I.
PARLOR IN A NEW YORK HOUSE.
ACT II.
LIBRARY AT DORINCOURT CASTLE —
EVENING.
(Six weeks elapse between Acts II and III.)
ACT III.
LIBRARY AT DORINCOURT CASTLE — AFTERNOON.

The Orchestra, under the direction of Mr. George Purdy,
will perform the following selections : —

1. Overture — Le Macon . . . . Auber.
2. Selection — Donna Juanita . . . . . . Suppe.
3. Gavotte (new) — La Petite Princesse . . .
   . . . . Boscowitch.
4. March — Dorscht . . . . Wiegand.

ACTING AND STAGE MANAGER . . . . Mr. HENRY M. PITT.

THE PIANOS FROM . . . . MESSRS. CHICKERING & SONS.
CABINET ORGANS FROM . . . . NEW ENGLAND ORGAN COMPANY.
GAS FIXTURES AND LAMPS FROM . . . . C. H. MCKENNEY & CO.
CARPETS AND RUGS FROM . . . . JOEL GOLDTHWAIT & CO.
FURNITURE FROM . . . . LAWRENCE, WILDE & CO.

AN ENTIRELY NEW PLAY

By BRONSON HOWARD, ESQ., author of Henrietta, Banker's Daughter,
etc., written expressly for the Boston Museum, to be
produced the TWELFTH OF NOVEMBER.

O O O how nice it all is, Dear Diary. It is settled about Fauntleroy and Papa. Mama and I will go back to Boston as the play will be at The Boston Museum. It will be called "Little Lord Fauntleroy" just like the book and not "The Real Little Lord Fauntleroy" like in London. Leo told me an interesting thing. A wicked man in London made a play of the story without telling Mrs. Burnett so she made the theter take it off the stage and put on the play she wrote herself in its place. That is why it was called "The Real Little Lord Fauntleroy." I don't understand about all this but Leo says it is important. It will help people who write stories and plays get paid for their work and that is a good thing, isn't it? Leo says I will like The Boston Museum Company as it is verry much loved in Boston and people will go there when they will not go to an other theter. I wonder why — Well, Mama and I leave tomorrow Papa to follow.

The Boston Museum Theatre, founded in 1841, and its stock company are famous in American theatre history. It was there on September 10, 1849 that Edwin Booth made his first appearance as Tressel in his father's production of *Richard III*. Admission was 25¢, with a limited number of seats at 50¢; children paid 12½¢. With the appearance of Junius Brutus Booth as the Duke of Gloster, established stars, among them Helena Modjeska, came to play at The Boston Museum. Its best-known manager was R. Montgomery Field. On the evening of June 1, 1903, The Boston Museum Theatre closed with a performance of Charles Frohman's Empire Theatre Company in *Mrs. Dane's Defense,* a play by Henry Arthur Jones.

Thomas Bailey Aldrich (1836–1907), American man of letters, best known for *The Story of a Bad Boy* 1870, *Marjorie Daw and Other People* 1873, and his verse.

Boston, Mass.
September 4, 1888

Dear Diary,

Here are three letters for you to keep for me. The first is from Mrs. Hall, the loverly lady who was a great singer and now teaches voice in Boston. She has a large pretty house and I like her. Mrs. Burnett is visiting her until the play is getting along well. Miss Mildred Aldrich is a kind lady who was at the party Mrs. Hall gave for Mrs. Burnett. It was a quiet tea-party and Mama and I were there also. Mama says Miss Aldrich is a lady who writes about actors and plays for the Boston newspapers. While the ladies were chatting Mrs. Hall gave me Tom Sawyer to look at so I curled up on the sofa and read. Later Miss Aldrich came and talked to me. Yesterday she sent me a book, The Story of a Bad Boy, by Mr. Thomas Bailey Aldrich. I must ask Mama if he is her Papa. I did ask Mama but she does not know.

206 Dartmouth Street
Boston, Mass.
Wednesday.

206 Dartmouth Street
Boston, Mass.
Sept. 6, 1888

My dear little Girl,

I found your pretty little letter waiting for me when I arrived yesterday morning, and as soon as I had read it I felt sure we should be friends. Every one tells me what a dear little Fauntleroy you will make, and I am looking forward with great pleasure to seeing you play to-morrow night. When you see in one of the boxes a little lady in a yellow brocade dress you will know who it is. Then after the play I shall try to see you for a few minutes, because I shall want to kiss you and tell you how pleased I am. I have no little girl of my own, but I have two boys, and one of them used to be just like Fauntleroy, and they both have always called me "Dearest". That is why I made Fauntleroy call his mother so. I know what a sweet little name it is. Mr. Gillett told me in New York how beautifully you play. I am sure he loves you as you say.

My dear little Elsie,

Your Fairy-Godmother is here and she has so much love for you that I know she will make you very happy and that there is something very nice in store for you.

You can come and see her tomorrow and I think she will go to the play tomorrow night.

We should have called to see your mother to-day, but the rain was too severe and we knew you would be away all day.

Mrs. Burnett will write you and say much sweeter things than I can.

My regards to your mother,
Your friend,
Edna Hall

Your affectionate friend
Frances Hodgson Burnett

(Right) Viola Allen

(Left) Elsie as
Little Lord Fauntleroy

The Boston Home Journal
Marlboro Building
Washington Street, Boston

Dear Elsie,

So you like "Tom Sawyer". I do, too. And as you like bad boy stories, perhaps you would like to read a story about a little boy I liked when I was a little girl. Here it is with my love.

Your friend,
Mildred Aldrich

Dear Diary,

The Boston Museum is verry nice but not as pretty as the Lyceum in New York. I love the Museum Company especuly Miss Viola Allen who is Dearest — that's my mother in the play, you know. She is verry beautiful. Before the play Mr. Frohman and Mr. Sothern sent me some roses and so did Leo. Mrs. Burnett read me a beautiful letter from Mr. Oliver Wendell Holmes about Little Lord Fauntleroy, which he verry much loved. She says she will ask Madame Hall to ask him to tea with Mama and me before we go to New York. I hope she will.

XXXXXXXX These are kisses for you, Diary, in case I haven't time to write you anymore before New York.

Dear Diary,

Mr. Frohman wanted a lot of pictures of me as Lord Fauntleroy. Mama is taking me to Mr. Sarony's studio. She says having your photograph taken is part of being an actress. After I become a Lord in the play I wear a velvet suit with a red sash and a hat with plumes. It is a loverly hat and with my riding suit I carry a real riding crop.

At the beginning of the play, Diary, I am a boy named

Cedric Errol living in New York City, and one of my best friends is Mr. Hobbs, the grocer. When I find out I have to go to England and be a Lord I don't want to tell him. This is what we say to each other in the scene —

"Mr. Hobbs, you said that you wouldn't have any lords sitting 'round on your cracker-barrels."

"So I did," says Mr. Hobbs. "And I meant it. Let 'em try it — that's all!"

"Mr. Hobbs, one is sitting on this barrel now!"

"Well, I'll be — jiggered!" says Mr. Hobbs.

He does forgive me for being a Lord in the end.

In Mrs. Burnett's book of Lord Fauntleroy there is a big dog. I was photographed with one just like him, but then in the end he wasn't in the play. The management was afraid he wouldn't behave properly on stage.

TOUR OF "LITTLE LORD FAUNTLEROY"
BY
Mrs. Frances Hodson Burnett

SEASON OF 1889-1890

SAMUEL FRENCH & SON
89 Strand, London
28 West 23d Street, New York City
Grand Opera House, New York City
AND PART OWNERS
Broadway Theatre, New York City

New York, Nov. 10th 1888

Mrs E. Leslie,

Madame:-

I have not notified you officially about your coming on to New York, so please accept this as said notification. We desire that Miss Elsie should have one entire week's rest before she rehearses, if she is able to do so. This course is forced upon us by the Society for the Prevention of Cruelty to Children, who have notified us that she must be examined by them before she will be permitted to play here. They did this on receiving letters from prominent people in Boston, stating that the child was much overworked. I hope this is not correct. When you arrive please notify me at once so that I can complete arrangements for having Miss Elsie examined by said Society. The rehearsals commence, I believe, at the Broadway Theatre next Monday

Yours truly,
J. N. French

TOUR OF "LITTLE LORD FAUNTLEROY"
By Mrs. Frances Hodgson Burnett
Season of 1889–1890
Samuel French & Son
89 Strand, London
28 West 23rd Street, New York City
Grand Opera House, New York City
And Part Owners
Broadway Theatre, New York City

New York
Nov. 10th, 1888

Mrs. E. Leslie,

Madame:–

I have not notified you officially about your coming to New York, so please accept this as said notification. We desire that Miss Elsie should have one entire week's rest before she rehearses, if she is able to do so. This course is forced upon us by the Society for the Prevention of Cruelty to Children, who have notified us that she must be examined by them before she will be permitted to play here. They did this on receiving letters from prominent people in Boston, stating that the child was much overworked. I hope this is not correct. When you arrive please notify me at once so that I can complete arrangements for having Miss Elsie examined by said Society. The rehearsals commence, I believe, at the Broadway Theatre next Monday.

Yours truly,
J. N. French

Little Lord Fauntleroy

We are back in New York now, dear Diary, but I can't begin rehearsals right away. Mama says I have to be examined by a society that protects children who work. There will be a doctor to look at me and the gentlemen will ask me about whether I get tired and things. I hope I answer right.

The examination is over. Dr. Quackenbush says I am a strong healthy girl but the Society thinks the part is too long for me to do eight times a week and another child must play part of the time. Oh, well!

The Broadway theatre is very big so we had lots of rehearsals but I didn't mind. A boy named Tommy Russell is rehearsing too. He will play the days I don't. We are good friends already.

Dear Diary,

Mama let me have this letter from dear Mr. Patten about the New York opening. I'm verry glad he liked it. Everybody seemed to.

133 West 47th Street

My dear Mrs. Lyde.

Wasn't it very delightful last night — I am certain that you are the proudest woman to be found anywhere, and you can well afford to be for Elsie's reception was a perfect ovation.

You know I have been trying for a long time to find "The Tower of London" for Elsie, but so far have not been sucsessful. I had intended sending Elsie a basket of flowers last night, but on second thoughts I ordered the book from London thinking she would appreciate that more. Mr. Chase has told me that he intends painting her portrait as Fauntleroy and if it turns out to his satisfaction he plans to give it to her which is certainly a fine thing for him to do. I met him at the theatre last night. Does Elsie dine with me Sunday evening? With kind regards to Miss Dora and yourself,

Faithfully
W. H. Patten.

The Tower of London by Harrison Ainsworth (1805–1882), English novelist, was so popular, it was published in several editions. The enchanting illustrations were the work of Cruikshank.

35

(Right) Elsie Leslie as Little Lord Fauntleroy, painted by W. M. Chase.
The portrait won the Silver Medal at the Paris Exhibition of 1900.
It hung on loan from Elsie for many years in the lobby of the Old Broadway Theatre.

133 West 47th Street
Wednesday evening.

Dear Elsie:—

Did you enjoy our little Sunday enough to try it again if Mama Lyde says "Yes"? If you did, we will go next Sunday to the studio of Mr. W. M. Chase, and I promise you a jolly good time. He has the finest studio in the city, a great big one, full of curious things and lots of pictures. You can dress yourself in silks and satins to your heart's content. There is something else in the studio you will like I am sure, though it is not very curious as you and I both looked at it once. It is Mr. Chase's little baby who is just beginning to toddle around. She dresses in a little black silk Japanese dress and looks very cunning. You are so fond of black silk dresses, what do you think of one made of fine Japanese silk with little fans embroidered at the bottom? I have a photograph of Mrs. Chase in one of these Japanese dresses holding the baby in her arms.

Then we can have lunch somewhere and get home in good season before we get tired out. Shall we try it? My friend, Mr. Walker, the editor of Cosmopolitan Magazine showed me what you wrote for him, and your funny drawing of the end of the world. But maybe you didn't intend it to be funny. Did you?

Good-bye, little Miss Letter Writer, tell Mama Lyde we behaved ourselves like good children when we went to the Church and she may let us go to the Chase.

faithfully
W. H. Patten

John Brisben Walker (1847–1931), American journalist and publisher. Founder and editor of Cosmopolitan Magazine (1889–1905) in which he published light fiction and articles dealing with the theatre in an informal manner.

Dear Diary,

Mr. Chase IS going to paint my portrait! I spose I will have to stand verry still while he paints. He is a verry famous artist.

Dear Diary,

Oh such an EXCITEMENT. The great Mr. Edwin Booth came to the play and just think he sent me this letter.

New York
Nov. 12, 1888

Dear Little Lady,

   Mr. Barrett and I were delighted with your charming performance of "Little Lord Fauntleroy" and we both wish you health and happiness.

Sincerely yours,
Edwin Booth

Here is another one from Mr. Booth —

Dec. 5th, 89
The Players
16 Gramercy Park.

My dear little friend,

   Do you think I could so soon forget the sweet little girl I had such a charming chat with the other day? Gracious! No indeed.

   But, dear Elsie, I'm afraid you won't like me when I tell you that I cannot (this week, at least) comply with your wish — much as I'd like to have a photograph of us. When I return to New York, two weeks hence, I will have more time, and if you are still here we can go to Sarony's studio and sit together for our picture. I am not able to go out today, and I have engagements for tomorrow which will prevent me from sitting to the artist before I return.

   Present my compliments to Mrs. Dodge and your sister — with love and kisses for your dear little self.

Edwin Booth

I would never have dared write to Mr. Booth and ask him to have his picture taken with me, Diary, if Mrs. Dodge hadn't speshully asked me to. I wonder if it will happen?

(Far right) Elsie with Edwin Booth

Dec. 5th, '89

My dear little friend

Do you think I could so soon forget the sweet little girl I had such a charming chat with t'other day? Gracious! No, indeed.

But, dear Elsie, I'm afraid you won't like me when I tell you that I cannot (this week, at least) comply with your wish — much as I'd like to have a photograph of us.

... and your sister — with love & a kiss for your dear little self. Edwin Booth

Edwin Booth
Elsie Leslie Lyde

Oh, Dear Diary,

It is loverly to have such pretty flowers and presents and I get so many. Another gift came to-day from a lady who came to tea a few days ago. It's a book and instead of a letter there is a poem that she wrote on the front page. The book is "The Birds' Christmas Carol" and here's the poem which I have copied for you.

> I met one day not so long ago,
> A dear little maid whose name you know.
> She's a ruby mouth, two sapphire eyes,
> A nice enough nose for a girl of her size.
> But oh! her curls!
> That sweetest of girls
> Had a head of adorable curls!
> Bright gold curls —
> The cunningest quirls!
> But afterwards I found, to my glad surprise,

> That neither the curls, nor the nose, nor the eyes
> Were of that little maiden the very best part,
> She had what was better, a golden heart,
> Heart of gold,
> For young and old,
> Filled with a wealth of love untold —
> Ah! If I were old
> And the world were cold
> I'd like to be loved with that heart of gold.

—Kate Douglas Wiggin

I wish I COULD be like that but Oh, dear . . . well, it's a loverly poem, isn't it?

The Birds' Christmas Carol is a classic children's story written by the well-known juvenile author, Kate Douglas Wiggin.

Tommy Russell. (At left) Tommy plays Little Lord Fauntleroy

Dear Diary,

Yes. Everybody in New York seems to like Little Lord Fauntleroy as much as they did in Boston. Isn't that wonderful?

I do like Tommy Russell. His sister is Miss Annie Russell, the actress. The day the play opened she gave each of us a big red apple which I thought was verry nice. Tommy said it was for luck. Mr. Gilmour looks verry fierce as the Earl but he is really a kind man and I love him. I miss my friends in the Boston company but I love this one too.

Tommy and I have a big dressing room and when I'm not playing he leaves me a letter on the mirror so I won't feel bad. We write to each other with soap on the looking glass and the cleaning woman washes it off. But we just laff. Mama says she is happy to be back in New York and I think Papa and Dora are also. O I forgot Tommy says he's glad he hasn't long curly hair like me that has to be brushed and combed a lot. He'd ruther wear a wig even if it's hot. Isn't that just like a boy? I have some pictures of him. One is in his wig and one's the way he looks every day.

Annie Russell (1864–1936), an enchanting actress, very popular and successful. After her retirement, she lived in Florida and built up the School of Drama at Rollins College.

Collette Clayton: Music Illustrator

Dear Diary,

I forgot to tell you that Dora took me to a speshul tea at Mrs. Dodge's and it was great fun. Mrs. Wiggin was there and so were Mr. Clarke and Mr. Birch, and Mrs. Rollins. It was verry exciting for Mrs. Wiggin sang a song she had composed to a poem Mrs. Rollins wrote for me and when it was over Mrs. Wiggin gave me the words and music just as she had written them down. Everybody clapped and Mr. Birch said, See here, Elsie, I want to do a drawing for you, and he did. He drew me and Lord Fauntleroy right on the music sheet. Dora has put it in a frame for me and it is now hanging by my desk. It is so pretty I shall always tresur it.

Dear Diary,

I must now tell you about the Bachelors. I came to know them after Mr. Sothern and I played Editha's Burglar for the Progress Club. I must esplain what the Progress Club is. It has some verry fine gentlemen in it over three hundred I think and all the members are bachelors who don't expect to marry. But once in a while one does get married and all the other gentlemen feel verry sad. They have their note paper edged with a black mourning band, even their hand-kerchiefs have a black border and when they go to the

---

William F. Clarke (1855–1935), long associated with Mary Mapes Dodge in the editorship of *St. Nicholas,* assumed full responsibility when Mrs. Dodge retired in 1905 and continued until 1927.

Alice Wellington Rollins was a minor poet and a popular member of literary circles at that time in Boston and New York.

Elsie Leslie, drawn by Reginald Birch

wedding of their old friend and member they wear black crape on their arm. And they shake hands with him and say Oh Brother, we are sorry for YOU and the married bachelor has to entertain the others with a dinner at Delmonico's. I must esplain something else. All the most of the Bachelors are rich but the dinners at Delmonico's cost such a lot it scares them and they are careful not to get married verry often. After I played Editha for them they gave me one hundred silver dollars and my darling little watch and one of them a verry special friend gave me my necklace of gold beads. The Bachelors are verry good boys and I think ever so much of them becoz they love me. Leo says the Progress Society is now the Bachelor's Club.

Dear Diary,

Here is my letter to thank the dear Bachelors for their Christmas presents. I wrote it at the theatre so Papa could mail it right away.

Dear Bachelors,

The lovely doll and the sled and the desk and the little chair all came just as Santa Claus told you and they are all loverly and I thank you verry verry much. All of my writing paper is not long enuf to write you my thanks. It would take paper as long as from 59th Street where the old Club House is to 5th Ave. where the new Club is but you must imagine that, for I can only write it on a sheet of paper that is only 7½ inches. I just mejured it. Please give my love to all the Bachelors and lots for my Burglar.

Your Little Friend,
Elsie Leslie

Dear Diary,

Mr. Birch came to tea. I showed him all my presents from the Bachelors. He thought they were grand, and he sat right down and drew this picture of me at my new desk.

And now here are some letters that will tell you more news, Diary.

Dear Old Elsie,

Thank you so much for your dear old telegram. The play went very well I think but I must do better in my part. I am a very wicked man this time — worse than the poor burglar and they say I was not quite wicked enough last night. But I WILL be wicked — you see if I don't!
God bless you, dear, and give you every happiness.
I hope you will have a jolly season.

With your burglar's love,
E. H. Sothern

Papa sent the telegram but I wrote this letter as well —

Dear Mr. Sothern,

It is just one year ago since we were playing the Burglar and now we are both playing lord parts. Do you like Chumley as well as the Burglar? I like Lord Fauntleroy better, it is longer you know. Love to all — speculy Mr. Archer. Is Dora a good girl, and does she do her part well?

43

Drawing by Reginald Birch of Elsie Leslie at the desk the Bachelors gave her.

I water colored the little picture on the front page but I did not draw it.

> *With love from your little friend,*
> *Elsie Leslie*

Dear Diary, Of course my dear Burglar answered at once.

> *Lyceum Theatre*
> *New York*

My dear old Elsie,

I received your very sweet letter tonight. It was delightful of you to think of me. I am so glad of your great success. I wish I could see your Lord, but I fear I shall not have a chance to do so. I like my Lord very much, but I still have some affection for the poor old Burglar, although you took all the piece away from me, no matter how hard I cried or how well I "burgled". Your sister Dora is a very good girl and has done her part splendidly. The water-color painting is lovely, and I think the little yellow girl is just like you. Mr. Archer sends his love to you and so do all the others, and even your old burglar sends a lot of love too —

> *God bless you dear —*
> *Yours*
> *E. H. Sothern*

Well, Mama took me to the matinee of Lord Chumley which is a verry funny play. I was so glad I could go as Tommy was taking my part that day. I laughed and laughed to see Mr. Sothern hopping about on one foot saying, Where is my slippah, where is my slippah? We had to hurry off after the play so Mama gave me a piece of paper to write him a letter to thank him for the tickets. I gave it to the usher to take back to my Burglar. The usher said Hullo, Elsie, it's good to see you in the Lyceum again and this made me verry happy. Dora looked beautiful as usual and I was verry proud of her Mama says she is pleased with us and it is fine that we are both in plays in New York now.

Here is another letter from Mr. Southern He wrote it at —

> *The Players*
> *16 Gramercy Park*

My dear Elsie,

What a big girl you are and what a good hand you write. I got the note after you had gone and I was very unhappy not to have seen you. I knew you were there and wanted you to come and tell me how you liked me or disliked me because you are my old "little girl" and I am always interested in your life and I am sure it is going to be great and fine for you. And nobody wishes for you happiness more than your "burglar" who hopes for you to be a great actress and a great woman.

My love to you my dear "old Elsie" —

> *Sincerely yours*
> *E. H. Sothern*

Lord Chumley, a play by H. C. De Mille and David Belasco, was another of the Lyceum Theatre Company plays in which E. H. Sothern was so successful.

I do hope I will never dissappoint my own dear first Burglar.

Lots of kisses for you, Diary X X X X X and for my Mr. Sothern.

Dear Mrs. Dodge,

The St. Nicholas magazine and the little Brownies came Monday afternoon   they are just loverly and I thank you verry verry much. I showed them all to Dearest and she thot they were loverly. O dear I must spell this word better I am now going to commence my letter to St. Nicholas. I do not have much time   I take a nap in the afternoon and that takes a long time. Remember me to all my new friends does Mr. Clarke write poems or stories? I think he looks as if he makes me think of a verry dear friend that I love verry much   he is the most trustable friend I have. I write to him often and he never allows the bad spelling in my letters to interfer with his love for me and I hope it will not interfer with yours and that you will always love your little friend.

Elsie Leslie

I thot I would have some fun, Diary. I would let my dolly write to Mrs. Dodge who might enjoy hearing from both of us. So I wrote this for my doll and put it in my letter to Mrs. Dodge at St. Nicholas.

Dear Mrs Dodge,

You must not expec verry much from my little daughter becoz she is only 5 years old but she teased me so hard to let her write to you that I could not say no, and you must excus her bad writing. I hope you will love her as much as she loves you becoz she is all the time talking about you and I hope you will get this letter becoz the child is so angshus to have you get it.

Your little friend
Elsie Leslie

Dear Mrs. Dodge,

I am Elsie's little dolly and I thot I would write you a letter becoz my Mama is going to write to you and I can put my letter in hers and I just wanted to write to you and say that I love you verry much becoz my Mama has told me all about you and I think you must be lovely.

Your faithful little friend,

Elsie's Little Girl.

My dear Elsie,

Your lovely letter and the very sweet note from your little daughter pleased me very much. I have a walking toy dog named Fido and he says he would like to write to your little girl. I hope you will not object to this as he is a very good dog, and is always most polite to persons smaller than he is. When you next come to see me, I shall be glad to introduce him to you. He is not on wheels, but he moves his legs beautifully when he walks, and turns his head with much feeling. Good-bye, dear Elsie.

Your sincere friend,
Mary Mapes Dodge

My dear very Littlest Miss Leslie:

Mrs. Dodge showed me the lovely letter you wrote her and I am astonished that a little girl of five years can write so nicely. I am only Mrs. Dodge's little toy dog Fido, and my paws are pretty stiff, so you must excuse my poor penmanship. Mrs. Dodge takes a great deal of pains in educating me, but as there is no Harvard Annex for dogs, I never can be very well educated. Still, a dog can be very agreeable without knowing Latin or Greek. I can nod my head and walk quite nicely. Can you? And do your eyes open and shut? Mine don't. I have a red collar with bells on it . . . I wish you and I could go to the park together if your dear Mama is willing. Mrs. Dodge sends her love to you, and says she loves you because you are Elsie's little girl. Goodbye. I forgot to say I have to be wound up with a key. Do you? Good-bye again. Give my love to your Mama. Does she have to be wound up before she plays Lord Fauntleroy?

Your little friend,
Fido.

Diary! This is SUCH fun, isn't it? But I do wish people would put the date on their letters. Maybe doggies never do. And I forget sometimes. Mama says she will tell Papa to get my next diary with the date printed on top of the page. This will help me notice pertically so that is a good idea. But how will it be if I can't get everything on one page?

Dear Diary,

Now I will tell you something else that is so nice. Leo takes me to the park as often as he can. I think it amuses him to see the children on their tricycles when he helps me across Fifth Avenue with mine. I am so glad to see him happy again becoz it has been so awful since dear Mrs. Gillette died last summer. Once in a while we talk about her. This is a kind of secret becoz sometimes he still feels so bad. Yesterday I asked him doesn't she love us just the same even if she is in heaven and he smiled and said Of course she does, dear.

It was VERRY cold anyway when we went to the park last time and I'd forgotten my mittens. So what does he do but lend me his big gloves. I didn't want to take them but he said his trouser pockets were VERRY warm so it would be all rite.

Leo admired my tricycle and said as he sat down on a bench Go it, Elsie. Let me see you fly down the hill. When I got back to him I was sort of tired so we just sat for a while on the nice bench in the sunshine and he told me a story about a doll in a book called Polly Cologne. He said Mrs. Diaz, the lady who wrote it was a friend of Mrs. Gillette's and would I like him to get a copy of it for me next time he was in a book store? I said Dear Leo, what can I say but yes even though you do too much for me alredy. Nonsense, he said, It's too cold to sit here any longer so shall we see if we can get it on the way home? Then he called a cabby and told him to take the tricycle to Mama with a note saying we had gone shopping but would be home soon. And off we went to a big store that just sold books and sure enuf they had it. so now I have another BOOK! Could anything be better than that, Diary?

I have started reading Polly Cologne between acts at the theatre. I like it verry much. Mama says it is all rite as long as I don't get too interested and miss my entrance cue.

Central Park, c. 1890

Culver Pictures

Dearest Diary, DEAREST DIARY, did you EVER hear of anything as loverly as this letter from Leo.

To my Little Love
With the Sunny Hair
    In Golden Strands,
I send a little glove
For her little pair
    Of Dainty Hands.

    Those precious hands so dear
    I could forever hold
      — Little Loves —
    I'd have them always near,
    I'd keep them from the cold,
      Without gloves.

    But 'twould be cruel to her
    To be before her face
      Without end;
    I'm sure she'd much prefer
    That now to take my place
      Gloves I Send.

When we are apart
In Far Distant Lands,
    — Which may be, —
Will the Little Heart
That owns the Little Hands
    Think of me?

    If we have to part
    Will the Chain of love
      Broken be?
    Will the Little Heart
    Referred to just above
      Care for me?

January · 1889

It's a poem, isn't it? It was in an envelope in a beautiful box that came by a Western Messenger this verry afternoon. AND WHAT WAS IN THE BOX? Of course. Gloves, gloves! The sweetest brown kid gloves you ever saw — lined with fur like Leo's grown-up ones but just my size. So my hands will never get cold again!

"I have a new coat too, with hat and muff to match."

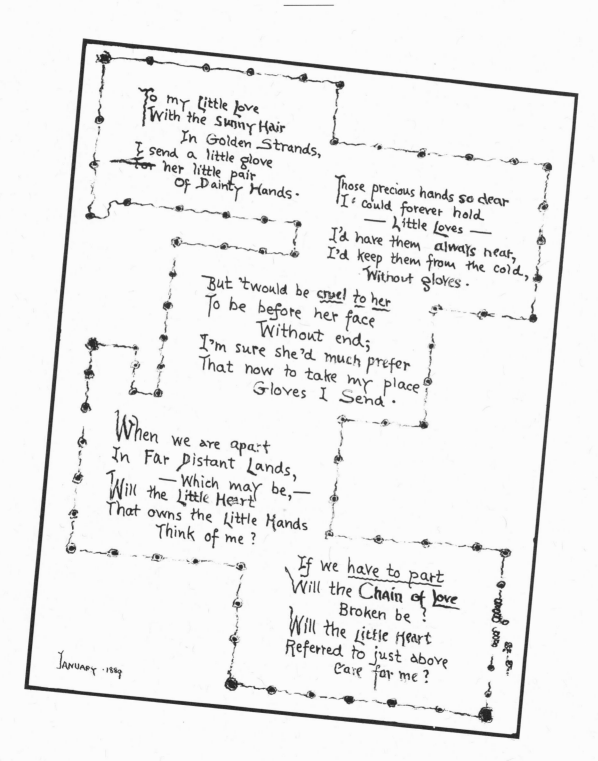

To my Little Love
With the Sunny Hair
   In Golden Strands,
I send a little glove
For her little pair
   Of Dainty Hands.

Those precious hands so dear
I could forever hold
   — Little Loves —
I'd have them always near,
I'd keep them from the cold,
   Without gloves.

But 'twould be cruel to her
To be before her face
   Without end;
I'm sure she'd much prefer
That now to take my place
   Gloves I Send.

When we are apart
In Far Distant Lands,
   — Which may be, —
Will the Little Heart
That owns the Little Hands
   Think of me?

If we have to part
Will the Chain of Love
   Broken be?
Will the Little Heart
Referred to just above
   Care for me?

January · 1889

Dearest Diary,

And now Papa has just met the Postman with the most preshus letter of all. The minute I saw the writing on the envelope, I knew it was from my DEAREST Mr. Jefferson.

Joseph Jefferson as Rip Van Winkle

Orange Island, La.
Feb. 14th, 1889

My dear Elsie,

I write to congratulate you on your recent great success.
You see your fame has reached me. And so now you are a bright little star illuminating thousands of happy mortals. I hear, too, that your good fortune has not spoiled you — that is the best news of all.

I am glad to know that you began your career upon the stage with me, though you owe me nothing, for you were so bright that teaching would have marred rather than benefited you. I am going to see you act as soon as I get the opportunity.

Good-bye — That you may always be happy and useful is the wish of your old friend,

J. Jefferson

I have a photograph of Mr. Jefferson which I treshur. It is from Rip van Winkle. This was when I first knew him. Mama says I wasn't even five years old but I remember.

Another loverly thing has happened, dear Diary. Leo brought Mr. and Mrs. Clemens and their three little daughters to the matinee of Little Lord Fauntleroy. They live in Hartford, Connecticut, and he is Mark Twain, the writer. Susy has golden hair like me but Clara is dark and they are all pretty. Jean is the youngest one and about the same size as me. Leo is going to take us all to lunch tomorrow at the Murray Hill Hotel. It is all arranged.

O tomorrow is almost over and Leo did and we had a wonderful time. Mr. Clemens told some VERRY funny stories and we had cream chicken and ice cream and cake. I told Mr. Clemens about Miss Aldrich saying she likes Tom Sawyer as much as I do so he said he would send me Huckleberry Finn — maybe next week. I am proud to think that I know Mr. Clemens who is a real writer. Dora gave me my beautiful copy of the Prince and the Pauper with lovely illustrations and it is my favorite book now even more than The Tower of London that Mr. Patten sent to London for. Mrs. Clemens says Hartford is not far away and Mama must bring me to visit the girls. Leo thot that this was fine and said I now have two homes in Hartford — his and the Clemens. I am so happy that Leo is here for a while but I don't know how long he will stay. And I'm glad he loves living at the Players Club where he has friends who love him. This will keep him from getting too lonesome.

Mr. Clemens didn't forget to send me the book, and here is what he wrote in it. I'm not quite sure what some of it means. I'll ask Leo and I'm sure he will esplane it to me.

Dear Elsie:
   This is the book I told you about last night at dinner. You'll find that what I said is true: it is one of the stateliest poems of modern times.

                            Sincerely yours
                            The Author

Jan. 3/89.

> Dear Elsie:
>   This is the book I told you about last night at dinner. You'll find that what I said is true: that it is one of the stateliest poems of Modern times.
>   Sincerely Your
>   The Author
> Jan. 3/89.

Dear Diary,

I feel verry gay indeed. What do you think? The Charity Ball at the Metropolitan Opera House on January the thirteenth is the grandest thing. It is to help pay for the German Opera AND Mama let me go with Dora for a little while becoz we had been asked to help sell flowers. I had lots of friends there like Mr. Frohman and Mr. Gerry and I made some more. I met Mr. and Mrs. Roosevelt who have a little girl like me. Her name is Eleanor. Now over a week later this letter has come.

> Feb'y 26/89
> Knickerbocker Club

My dear Elsie,

As I could not get you the bonbons the night of the fancy ball I send you a little box of them now. I hope you will enjoy them. My little girl sends her love to you. And with the same from Mrs. Roosevelt and myself, I am,

> *Yours very truly*
> *Elliott Roosevelt*

Don't forget you promised to send me your picture with your name written on the back —

Well, Mama chose the picture and I wrote carefully — really carefully so now I have this letter:

> Feb'y 28/89
> 56 West 57th Street.

Dear little Elsie —

Your note and the photograph and the well written name signed on the back I got to-day — It was my birthday so I took it as a great compliment. The baby says if you will lunch with her on any Sunday she will be so pleased to see you again, so do come if you can.

> *Yours truly*
> *Elliott Roosevelt*

I want to go verry much, Diary, Mama says she will arrange it as soon as she can.

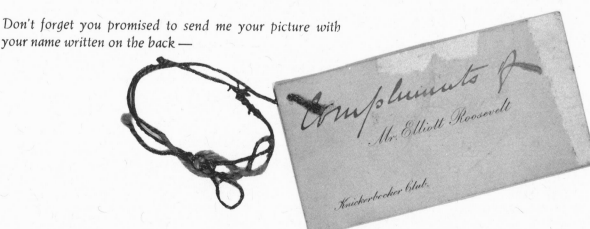

Eleanor Roosevelt as a child with her father Elliott Roosevelt
and her brother Hall

Feby 28/89.
56 WEST 37TH STREET.

Dear little Elsie —
Your note and
the photograph, and
the well written name
signed on the back
I got to day — It
was my birthday
so I took it as a
great compliment

Yours truly
Elliott Roosevelt

230 West 42d Street

"The Percival"   City

Oh, dear Diary,

It is beginning to get hot and the theters will be closing. Saturday will be my last time as Fauntleroy as Mama says I must have a long rest. After it I hope I can go to school like other girls do. Tommy will take my part in New York for a short time before he goes on tour with the play. I am glad becoz he wants to do this verry much. He has just sent me a paper doll and this dear letter. I shall keep them always. I am happy that this letter won't get washed off the dressing room mirror the way our soap letters were. Mama has got another box of Fauntleroy paper for Tommy so I hope he will write often. He will have to use real stamps even though they are not as funny as the one he drew for the envelope of this letter.

I am glad to have this darling writing paper. Several more boxes were sent me by my friends the L. C. Prang Co. This is a big company in Boston and they have made writing paper and playing cards too with pictures of me as Little Lord Fauntleroy on them. My dear friend Schuyler Mathews, the artist, suggested this to Mr. Prang and made the drawings for them. Mr. Prang has made copper plates from the drawings, and now he can print as many as children want to order, and he doesn't need the original drawings any more. So Mr. Mathews says I can have the drawings to keep, and Mr. Prang says when I need more paper all I have to do is ask and Presto! they will arrive. I love the Prang Co. verry much and Mr. Mathews too.

Dearest Diary,

At last the good old summer time is close at hand. How I love the long warm days out of doors. Now I can forget about all the hussle and bussle in town. Once we are off to Road's End, our summer cottage in Poultney, Vermont, I can really believe it is vacation time.

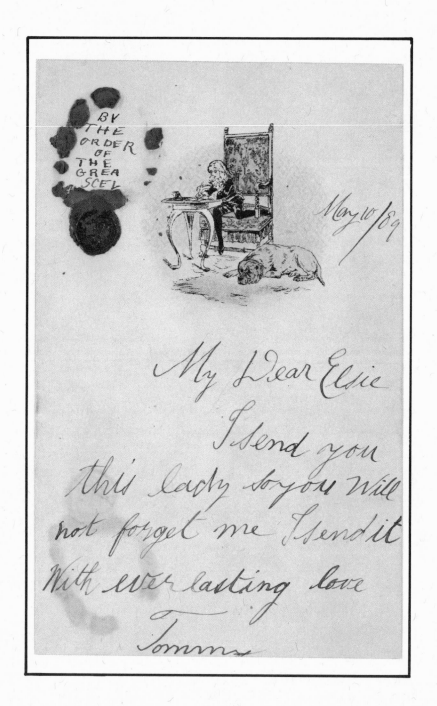

Road's End, the Lyde family's summer cottage in Vermont

Once we were in the train such happiness began. Papa was soon nodding over his newspaper and Mama started a letter to Dora who is still in New York. And I spent the time looking out the window as we sped along. I thot about Tommy going to so many strange places where thousands of children will see Fauntleroy and how he will enjoy it. Well, lots of children saw me act in it in Boston and New York so it's only fair for him to play it in other cities.

Finally we are here. And now I must tell you about yesterday which was the wonderfulest thing of all. When the train arrived at Poultney, Mr. Johnston, our station master,

was there waving his hat and Mr. Bates was there with the carriage waiting for Mama and Papa to get in and Mr. Lynch was also there with the carriage cart to take the luggage AND right behind him who should there be but Artie Burdick with the GREAT SURPRISE, the one thing I've been wishing for, the cunningest little wicker pony cart you ever saw! It looks sort of like a wicker laundry basket as it's round and there is a little door in the back and when you open it a little step drops down so you can get in without any trouble and the seats are covered with brown leather like the harness and all. I was so excited I almost forgot to hug Lolo who was twitching his ears to show me how

proud he was. I don't wonder for he's only a donkey and not a Shetland pony at all. Never mind, he's named for a verry famous pony in one of my most favorite stories called Jackanapes.

Papa came over and said Elsie, don't you want to get in and let Artie drive you home? Of course I did and as we rattled along behind the carriage I thot how wonderful it is to be surprised with such a gift. And it's not even my birthday. Mama and Papa had Mr. Bates buy it for me from a gentleman in Castleton. Artie says it's good Lolo is a smallish donkey and the pony cart is just the right size for him. It is big enough to hold three or four children and Artie says he's sure Lolo will be proud to haul us about. Later on I hope Mama will let me drive myself and I think

she will if Artie or one of the older children is with me. O that will be wonderful!

I do so love it here and more every time I come back. There are plenty of children to play with and there's fishing and tree climbing and when I go to the Burdick farm there are many animals to play with. Artie is almost thirteen and he and his sister Louise are two of my verry best friends. They never forget me even when I am away so much.

When I am not doing any of these things I can lie in the hammock on the porch with a book. Road's End is VERRY heaven.

WELL, Dear Diary, can you believe this? There is even better news! Mr. Clemens HAS GRANTED MY WISH. He has agreed to have The Prince and the Pauper made into a play! AND it will be fixed so I can play both parts!! What do you think of that? Leo says he knew about it but he did not say one word becoz he wanted Mama to tell me. Leo knows Mrs. Richardson who is making the book into a play. She has done lots of work for my deary Mr. Frohman who will produce the play and Leo says she is verry clever. No. Leo didn't write this great news in a letter — he is HERE! I am so happy about everything I cannot describe my feelings.

Leo is writing a play himself. He gets up very early and makes himself some breakfast before he goes up to my playhouse where he is doing it. My playhouse is across the creek quite a way up the hill in the woods. Leo says he loves this so much becoz it's so verry quiet and peaceful. It has always been a sort of secret place for Dora and me to practice our parts and not disturb anyone. And now it's helpful to Leo and I'm so glad. He works verry hard I think but he lets me come up for him when Mama says he must stop for a meal. Yes, we love having him here and Mama says it is better for him to keep busy than to be sad but I'm afraid he is verry sad sometimes.

Abby Sage Richardson (1837–1900), compiler, editor, and dramatist best known for *Familiar Talks on English Literature, Abelard and Heloise: A Medaeval Romance, Songs from the Old Dramatists,* and her dramatization of Mark Twain's *The Prince and the Pauper.*

Well, it was joyful that he was here for my birthday which was the fourteenth of August. So I am now nine! After breakfast he was mejured on the sitting room door like I am every year. He thot his name would look strange so far above mine becoz he is so much taller than me. But he wrote it anyway and it looks grand. I wonder how tall I will get to be when I am grown up. After Leo had done this he looked down and smiled and said I must learn to BE tall and walk like a prince. So I go up and down stairs with a book on my head several times a day. Also, Leo and I play fencing the way we think little Prince Edward learned it.

It is great fun but it is hard work too. Leo says he's not the best fencing teacher in the world. He says he knows more about writing about fencing than doing it, but I think he is a wonderful teacher besides being my most preshus friend.

Alas, dear Diary, so many loverly times come to an end. And now my heart sinks at the thot of my holiday ending. Indeed, the leaves are turning early this year and watching them I knew we must soon leave this loverly place. Mr. Bates says he will take care of the horse and Lolo and help Papa get things put away before the first big frost. We do have such kind neighbors. In a few days now Mama and Dora and I are going back to New York to begin work on "The Prince and the Pauper" which Mr. Belasco is going to direct for Mr. Frohman. Dora is going to be the Princess Elizabeth. After we get settled in town Papa will shut up the cottage and come as soon as he can. I hate to leave becoz I love the Autumn here almost as much I love getting up the play.

I hope Mr. Clemens will be there often while we are rehearsing but Leo said he did not think so. Leo says Mr. Clemens is always saying he doesn't know anything about plays and that he wants to see "The Prince and the Pauper" when it is all done. Leo says Mr. Clemens likes the fun but not the work. I think Leo was only joking. He has now gone and I miss him verry much indeed   we all do. I was so down hearted when we drove him to the train that he took my hand and said, "Cheer up, Elsie, time passes quickly and it won't be long until we meet again in town and go to The Murray Hill for supper." So I didn't cry and now I keep telling my self, "Pull up, Elsie, pull up, Elsie or you'll never be able to do such a big thing as the loverly play."

Dear Diary,

I can't tell you how hard we are all working on The Prince and the Pauper   indeed every one tries so hard to please Mr. Belasco who is I think verry nice in his heart but he is verry verry stern and that frets some of the others in the company. Anyhow, what with it all, it was indeed fine that I have had such a grand surprise. It has made me so VERRY VERRY happy. So here is the story of the wonderful pair of slippers   this is told in the next two letters. The one from Mr. Clemens was in the box that came from him by American Express. It says:

Hartford
Oct 5, '89.

Dear Elsie:

The way of it was this. Away last spring, Gillette and I pooled intellects on this proposition: to get up a pleasant surprise of some kind for you against your next visit — the surprise to take the form of a tasteful and beautiful testimonial of some sort or other, which should express some-

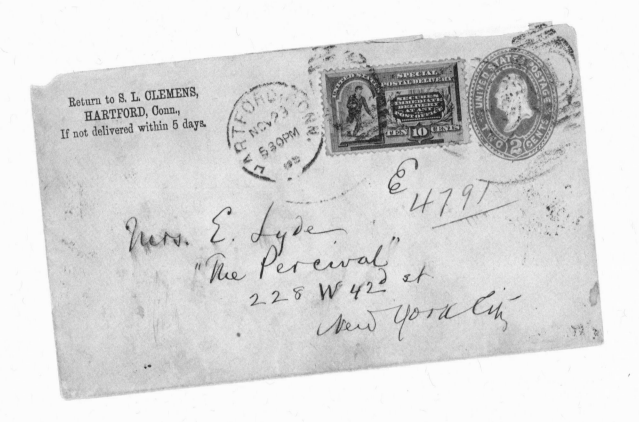

Return to S. L. CLEMENS,
HARTFORD, Conn.,
If not delivered within 5 days.

Mrs. E. Lyde
"The Percival"
228 W 42d st
New York City

what of the love we felt for you. Together we hit upon just the right thing — a pair of slippers. Either one of us could have thought of a single slipper, but it took both of us to think of two slippers. In fact, one of us did think of one slipper, and then, quick as a flash, the other thought of the other one. It shows how wonderful the human mind is. It is really paleontological: you give one mind a bone, and the other one instantly divines the rest of the animal.

Gillette embroidered his slipper with astonishing facility and splendor, but I have been a long time pulling through with mine. You see, it was my very first attempt at art, and I couldn't rightly get the hang of it at first. And then I was so busy that I couldn't get a chance to work at it, at home, and they wouldn't let me embroider on the cars: they said it would make the other passengers afraid. They didn't like the light that flared into my eyes when I had an inspiration. And even the most fair-minded people doubted me when I explained what it was I was making — especially the brakemen. Brakemen always swore at it, and carried on the way ignorant people always do about art. They wouldn't take my word that it was a slipper: they said they believed it was a snow shoe that had some kind of a disease.

But I have pulled through, and within twenty-four hours of the time I told you I would — day before yesterday. There ought to be a key to the designs, but I haven't had time to get one up. However, if you will lay the work before you with the forecastle pointing north I will begin at that end and explain the whole thing, layer by layer so that you can understand it.

I began with that first red bar, and without ulterior design, or plan of any sort — just as I would begin a Prince and Pauper or any other tale. And mind you, it is the easiest and surest way, because if you invent two or three people and turn them loose in your manuscript, something is bound to happen to them — you can't help it, and then it will take you the rest of the book to get them out of the natural consequences of the occurrence, and so, first thing you know, there's your book all finished up and never cost you an idea. Well, the red stripes, with a bias stitch, naturally suggested a blue one with a pendicular stitch, and I slammed it in, though when it came daylight I saw it was green — which didn't make any difference because green and blue are much the same anyway, and in fact from a purely moral point of view are regarded by the best authorities as identical. Well, if you will notice, a blue perpendicular stitch always suggested a ropy red involved stitch, like a family of angleworms trying to climb on top of each other to keep warm — it would suggest that, you know, without the author of the slipper having to think of it at all.

Now at that point, young Dr. Root came in, and of course he was interested in the slipper right away, because he has always had a passion for art himself, but he has never had a chance to try, because his folks are opposed to it and superstitious about it, and done all they could to keep him back; and so he was eager to take a hand and see what he could do. And it was beautiful to see him sit there and tell Mrs. Clemens what had been happening while we were off on summer vacation, and hold the slipper up to-

ward the end of his nose, and forget the sordid world, and imagine the canvas was a "subject" with a scalp wound, and nimbly whirl in that lovely surgical stitch, which you see there — and never hesitating a moment in his talk except to say "Ouch" when he stuck himself, and then going right on again as smooth and easy as nothing. Yes, it was a charming spectacle. And it was real art, too, realistic; just native untaught genius; you can see the very scalp itself, showing through between the stitches.

Well, next I throw in that sheaf of green rods which lictors used to carry before the Roman Consuls to lick them when they didn't behave, — they turned blue in the morning, but that is the way green always acts.

The next week, after a good rest, I snowed in sea of frothy waves, and set that yellow thing afloat in it and those two things that are skewered through it. It isn't a home plate, and it isn't a papal tiara with the keys of Saint Peter; no, it is a heart — my heart — with two arrows stuck through it — arrows that go in blue and come out crimson — crimson with the blue drops in that heart, and gladly shed for love of you, dear.

Now, then, as you strike to the south'ard and drift along down the starboard side, and abaft the main top gallant scuppers, you come to the quarter-deck which runs the rest of the way on to the jumping-off place. In the midst of the blue you will see some big red letters — M.T.; and westward, over on the port side, you will see some more red letters — to E.L. Aggregated, these several groups of letters signify, Mark Twain to Elsie Leslie. And you will notice that you have a gift of art for yourself, for the southern half of the L., embroidered by yourself is as good as anything I can do, after all my experience.

There, now you understand the whole work. From a professional point of view I consider the Heart and Arrows by all odds the greatest triumph of the whole thing: in fact, one of the ablest examples of civil engineering in a beginner I ever saw — for it was all inspiration, just lightning-like inspiration of the moment. I couldn't do it again in a hundred years, — even if I recover this time and get just as well as I was before. You notice what fire there is in it — what rapture, enthusiasm, frenzy, what blinding explosions of color. It is just like a "Turner" — that is what it is. It is just like his "Slave Ship", that immortal work. What you see in the "Slave Ship" is a terrific explosion of radiating rage and fragments of flaming crimson flying from a common center of intense yellow which is in violent commotion — in so much that a Boston reporter said it reminded him of a yellow cat dying in a platter of tomatoes.

Take the slippers and wear them next to your heart, Elsie dear; for every stitch in them is a testimony of the affection which two of your loyalest friends bear you. Every single stitch cost us blood. I've got twice as many pores in me as I used to have; and you would never believe how many places you can stick a needle into yourself until you go in to the embroidery line and devote yourself to art.

Do not wear these slippers in public, dear; it would only excite envy, and like as not, somebody would try to shoot you.

Merely use them to assist you in remembering that among the many, many people who think all the world of you is your friend,

Mark Twain

I sat right down and wrote to him.

"THE PERCIVAL"
APARTMENT HOTEL,
228, 230, 232 West 42d Street,
NEW YORK CITY.

PANNACI'S HOTEL,
SEA BRIGHT, N. J.

NEW YORK, N. Y., Oct 9th. 1889.

My dear Mr Clemens

The slipper the long letter and all the rest came this afternoon I think thay are splendid and shall have them framed and keep them among my very most prechus things. I have had a great many nice things given to me and people often say very pleasant things but I am not quite shure thay always mean it or that thay are as trustable as you and "Leo" and I am very shure thay would not spend their prechus time and shed their blood for me so you see that is one reson why I will

top left corner of this letter
To my loyal frend
Mark Twain
from his little frend
(over)

New York
October 9, 1889

My dear Mr. Clemens:

The slippers the long letter and the rest came this afternoon, I think they are splendid and shall have them framed and keep them among my verry most preshus things. I have had a great many nice things given to me and people often say verry pleasant things but I am not quite shure they always mean it or that they are as trustable as you and "Leo" and I am verry shure they would not spend their preshus time and shed their blood for me   so you see that is one reason why I will think of two great big men like you and "little Willie" (that is what "Leo" calls himself to me) imbroidering a pair of slippers for a little girl like me of course you have a great many large words in your letter that I do not quite understand. One word comencing with P. has fifteen letters in it and I do not know what you mean by pooled unless you mean that you and Leo put your two minds together to make the slippers which was verry nice of you both   I think you are just right about the angle worms they did look like that this summer when I used to dig them for bate to fish with   please tell Dr. Root I will think of him when I look at the part he did — the surgicle stich I mean   I hope you will be quite well and strong by the time you get this letter as your were before you made my slipper   it would make me verry sad if you were to be ill. Give my love to Mrs. Clemens, Susie, Clara and Jean — I know and you know — and Vix and all of my Hartford friends tell Jean I wish I was with her and we would have a nice jump in the hay loft. When you come to New York you must come and see me   then we will see about those big words   my address is up in the top corner of this letter.

To my loyal friend
Mark Twain
from his little friend
Elsie Leslie Lyde

P.S. Not Little Lord Fauntleroy now but Tom Canty of Offal Court and little Prince Edward of Wales.

Dearest Diary,

WHAT a thing it was doing The Prince and the Pauper, about which Mr. Belasco seemed verry nervous. Some of the actors became upset and dishearted as the rehearsals went on but I didn't. I love the play too much for that. I reely enjoyed it all but I did get a verry bad cold. Dora said maybe it was becoz I didn't get enuf rest and also becoz I esplained to Mama that when I was Tom Canty i MUST NOT wear stockings and shoes becoz he did not have any. Mrs. Richardson told me people wouldn't think it VERRY NICE for a little girl to show her legs. I mean her bare skin but I said I wasn't a little girl when I was Tom Canty. Mama was inclined to agree with the others becoz she thot it was important for people to think I was a verry well brot up child so I said I did not think that had anything to do with this and she finally let me ask Mr. Belasco what HE thot. So I asked him verry politly if we could talk about something I wanted to know. He was so nice and we had a talking like Papa and I do sometimes and I esplained to him that Tom Canty was awful poor and had no warm close just rags and that he MUST be barefooted   the story said so AND he said I was quite rite and it should be that way and we must hope that I didn't get sick if it was cold on stage so I said I was verry strong anyway. Mama was quite upset so dear Mr. Frohman had a kind doctor from the Children's Hospital there all the time and he went with us to Philadelphia to look after me.

The night we opened in Philadelphia everybody felt nervous as one does on the first night of a new play. My knees were knocking together but I KNEW I could do it and by

BROADWAY THEATRE,

39th Street and Broadway, New York.

FRANK W. SANGER, - - - - MANAGER.

Commencing Monday, January 20, 1890.

EVERY EVENING AT 8 O'CLOCK.

MATINEES WEDNESDAYS AND SATURDAYS,

DANIEL FROHMAN'S PRODUCTION

—OF—

THE PRINCE AND THE PAUPER,

(WITH ELSIE LESLIE.)

Dramatized from MARK TWAIN'S Story

—BY—

ABBY SAGE RICHARDSON.

UNDER THE STAGE DIRECTION OF DAVID BELASCO.

the time we got to New York I was fine I mean I felt just fine. I am VERRY happy too that my two dear friends, Mister Vanderfelt and Mister Elliot are in the company. Mr. V. is Miles Hendon and Mr. E. is The Earl of Hertford and they look splendid in their costumes. When I am Tom Canty, Miss Annie Mayor is my mother and Dora looks so loverly as the Princess Elizabeth. The New York opening was at The Broadway Theater which I know well by now. It was on January 20th as you will see from the booklet about the play. I am so proud of it and am glad that it fits in your pages, Dear Diary. The opening in New York seems like a wonderful dream now. The hardest part was having to stand in front of the curtain at the end while Mr. Clemens made a speech. Mr. Share who is the Art Director for the New York Herald was there and he made a sketch of us which is in the paper. Mama and Dora said I would not like it it looks like Mr. Clemens but I look funny but I don't care if it makes people come to the play.

When I am playing Prince Edward I do try to stand VERRY tall and remember everything Leo taught me about fencing last summer in Vermont.

E. H. Vanderfelt, a well-known Shakespearean actor and the first to play Miles Hendon in *The Prince and the Pauper.*

Henry Pruett Share (1853–1905), newspaper artist noted for his ability to get a likeness quickly, and one of the many illustrators for *Around the World with Grant* by John R. Young.

The Prince and the Pauper

Here I am as the Prince who wasn't ever allowed to go barefoot.

In this picture I am Tom Canty WITH BARE LEGS.

Dear Diary,

Oh dear the news is rather sad. Mr. Frohman has decided to take The Prince and the Pauper on tour. We will go to Chicago next week. It will seem strange but I have lots of friends there and Mama says she is sure the people in Chicago will appreciate the play.

We are now there and I have seen many dear friends and every one is so kind. And the best thing is that lots of children have come to see the play and they all love it just as I knew they would.

Chicago is a big city. I remember post cards Tommy Russell sent me from there. I am sad he is not here now but I like the understudy. She is verry good in the part, I think and she is smallish but verry pretty. She is not a child but a young lady maybe twenty I think and her name is Miss Fanny Ward. Mr. Booth is also in Chicago as you will see from this letter from him. Mama says when we go to see him we must stay only a little while becoz we must not tire him.

Fanny Ward (1872–1952), born Fannie Ward Buchanan, was Elsie Leslie's understudy in Daniel Frohman's production of *The Prince and the Pauper*. She went on to become a successful actress in London and New York and married "Diamond Joe Lewis," London financier and mining businessman associated with Cecil Rhodes.

Fanny Ward

Grand Pacific Hotel
Chicago, Illinois
March 16, 1890

My dear little Elsie,

I am sorry I cannot see your performance and which I want so much to do but when I act at night I am obliged to shut myself up all afternoon for a rest. I am not quite as young as you are, and require all the quiet and repose I can get before I go to work. Saturdays, of course, I have to suffer.

Any day before two o'clock I'll be happy to receive your Mama and yourself, if you will let me know the day previous when it will be convenient for you to call.

I hope you are having as splendid a success with the Prince as you did with the Lord.

Take care of your health and don't work too hard. Bless you, dear.

Your friend,
Edwin Booth.

ELSIE LESLIE'S DOG.

Another dear friend lives here. This is my dear Mr. Edward C. Freiberger who has known Dora and me ever since we were verry young as he was such a good friend of our parents. He is interested in music and the theter and he is also a close friend of Mr. Eugene Field, the poet. Soon after we arrived Mr. Freiberger brought Mr. Field to tea and this was indeed nice. Mr. Freiberger comes and takes me and my dog Todkins walking whenever he can. Here is a story he wrote about us for a Chicago paper. He and Mr. Field thought others might enjoy hearing the tale of the christning of Todkins. I think it is verry funny, don't you, dear Diary?

Little Elsie Leslie gave a private party last Sunday. She was the party of the first part, while her pet doggie was the party of the second part. The party depended largely upon the second part. Provided he did not howl! Provided he did not yell! Provided he did not bite! Provided also that he

Eugene Field (1850–1895), American poet and journalist well known for his column in the Chicago *Daily News,* "Sharps and Flats." *The Tribune Primer, A Little Book of Western Verse,* and *Love Affairs of a Bibliomaniac* are published collections of his newspaper verses. The creator of many popular and sentimental children's poems, he is remembered best for "Little Boy Blue" 1889.

would not kick or in any other manner, undoglike or dog-like vociferously or wildly attempt to enjoy his little bark all by himself. Therefore it was a surprise party. The Dog was the last to be invited, for dear little Elsie did not know under what name the dog could be invited. He had no name, notwithstanding the dear little girl and the little dog had kept company for something like a year. So, before the party occurred, the dog was christened; ceremony private, admission by card only. The dog is to go through life and pick bones and things under a triple cognomen. It is to be Todkins Tudor Lyde. History proclaims not where, and when, and under what circumstances little Elsie secured these names. The second name would indicate that possibly the dog was related to Lady Grey, a bright and promising cat once owned by Mark Twain. (The last name is Elsie's own family name.) The dog is not even English, you know. He does not even attend George Keenan's lectures, for the reason that he is a pure Russian pug, very small, very short, but otherwise pleasing to the eye. He is now a year and a half old and has never had a name. The rumor that he went into bankruptcy and lost his name by order of the court is absolutely false. Like Elsie Leslie he is fond of chocolate cream puffs. Elsie eats them everyday. Tuesday, April 1, she didn't eat any. She tried to and failed. The bad cook at the Leland Hotel and the bad people who sat at the table with her entered into a conspiracy and took the bad waiter into their confidences and played a bad April fool joke on Elsie. The cream cakes were such only in name. They had no cream in them. They were filled with cotton. She had been thinking all day long how she might fool all the wicked people she knew. But she never thought they might fool her. But they did. At first she was amazed. Then somebody looked at somebody else. Only the bad newspaper fiend at the table looked her in the face. Then she saw the point and laughed until her lovely hair fell over her face covering it with a golden eclipse. Then when she had finished laughing she exclaimed, "Waiter, please wrap these cakes in paper for me. I'll take them to the theatre and fool Mr. Elliot." And she did.

The christening ceremony occurred at the Leland Hotel, in Elsie's room, last Sunday afternoon. Little Elsie had prepared the invitations herself. Attached to a golden scroll some six inches long, was a sheet of linen paper. The invitation said:

> "Mr. ___ ___'s presence is desired
> at the christening of Miss Todkins Tudor Lyde,
> at the Leland Hotel, Sunday April 6 1890,
> at 1:30 p.m.
> —Elsie Leslie Lyde."

In the lower left hand corner was a pretty design in gold which Miss Elsie said was the dog's court of arms.

Miss Todkins Tudor Lyde received a number of presents, such as a silver bowl from Elsie, a silver plate from one of her girl friends and also a harness from Mr. Charles Metcalf. The dog, a cunning and intelligent little animal, was attired in a coat of white ribbon, tied round his neck, while his breath came in short pants. Otherwise, all went off with grace and charm.

Dearest Diary,

We are back in dear old Boston but not at the Museum where we played Little Lord Fauntleroy. This time it is the Hollis Street Theatre. I remember how big it seemed to me when we went there with Editha's Burglar. Of course I was smaller then.

Now another loverly story. Here are two letters for you to keep for me. They are from the little blind girl Helen Keller.

Helen Keller and Anne Sullivan, 1890

So. Boston, Mass.
April 23rd 1890

My dear Little Friend,

You will be surprised to receive a letter from a little girl whom you do not know but I hope you will be glad that I think about you and love you. I want very much to touch you because I cannot go to the theater and see you play for I am very blind, and I could not hear your voice because I am deaf. It will make me very happy if you will let me come to see you. My teacher has told me about you, and I have read little Lord Fauntleroy with my fingers. I thought Cedric was a lovely little boy. I should love dearly to see you dressed like a beautiful prince. Will you please let me come to see you. My teacher has told me about you, and studying. Now Little Elsie, good-bye. I shall wait eagerly to hear from you. I am learning to speak with my mouth. I can say Elsie.

Lovingly your Little Friend,
Helen A. Keller

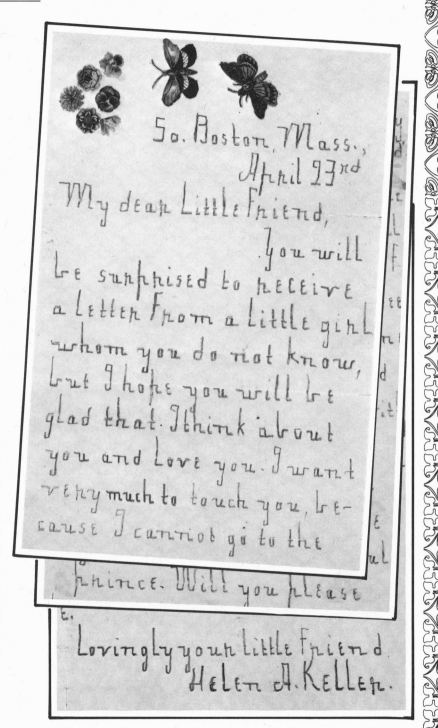

South Boston, Mass.,
April 29, 1890

My sweet Little Friend,

I thought I would write you a letter this beautiful and sunny morning, and tell you how much I enjoyed seeing you last Sunday. You cannot imagine how happy it made me to touch your lovely hair, and sit beside you in the chair. Are you very glad because you can make so many people happy? I am so delighted that I can go to the theater! I have never been for Teacher says I would not enjoy it, but I shall, and you will let me see you dressed like a prince, I should like to be a lovely princess. I have invited some of the teachers to go with me so that they can tell the little blind children all about the play. I have told them that you and your kind friends are coming to see them. They clapped their hands for joy. They will sing for you and recite. I love you very dearly, Little Elsie, because you are such a kind little girl. Will you write to me sometimes when you are not busy? If you would like to. Please give my love to your 'Dearest' and your dear sister Dora and Mr. Spaulding and all of your friends. My teacher wants me to thank you and your friends for her share of the pleasure. Now my sweet little Elsie, good-bye until tomorrow. I am so eager for tomorrow to come I can hardly wait patiently.

Your loving little friend,
Helen A. Keller

Miss Sullivan or "Teacher," the name Helen Keller gave to Anne Sullivan, was her tutor. Though her marriage to John Albert Macy in 1905 ended in separation, Anne Sullivan retained her married name of Macy and continued, until her death, to act as companion to Helen Keller.

After the matinee on Saturday, little Helen was brought backstage to see me. Mama was afraid that it would upset me to see a blind child but it did not. She was so sweet and we liked each other at once. Last Sunday afternoon Dr. Brooks took Mama and me out to the Perkins Institute where Helen was waiting for us in the parlor. Perkins Institute is a wonderful place where blind children and others are taught to read and write and everything. The grounds are beautiful and it is so sad that the dear blind people cannot see the loverly green grass and the flowers and trees. Dr. Brooks took us in his carriage and made it all so pleasant and he insisted that Miss Sullivan should bring Helen to the theter becoz her heart is set upon it. I don't see how anyone could refuse Helen anything. Even if she is just a little girl I think she is one of the bravest people in the world, don't you? Miss Sullivan told me that Little Lord Fauntleroy was the first book that Helen read by herself and Helen said how VERRY much she loved it and that she loves The Prince and the Pauper almost more now that she is a little older and is studying history.

Her letters are so preshus I shall keep them forever.

Dear Diary, This will be a verry short letter for we are doing one night or one week stands in and around New York City. That is I think the Bronx is in New York. We have also played lots of places in New England. When we were in Hartford we stayed with the Clemens. Jean Clemens and I were playing in the hayloft one day when Mrs. Clemens came to tell me it was time for me to go to the matinee. For the only time in my whole life I said, "I don't want to go." "Why, Elsie," said Mr. Clemens, "some little girls would give anything to be an actress, and think how many people are depending on you to be there."

On hill beside
Mark Twain's house

(Above) Mark Twain.
(Above, right) Elsie on her sled
at Mark Twain's home

Ode.

To Elsie Leslie.

I'll be your friend, your thrall, your knave,
I'll be your elder brother;
I'll be for love your very slave,
Or anything you'd druther.

Mark.

Hartford, March 5, 1890.

Mark Twain's home in Hartford, Connecticut

"I don't care," I said. "I'm going to stay here with Jean." "My goodness, you are a stubborn little rat," he said. This made me cry and he said, "Elsie, will you go if I take you myself?" Of course I went and he was so kind and funny I forgot I hadn't wanted to go. And, dear Diary, I didn't want him to think I was a stubborn little rat.

We are still playing, Diary, and between shows I have enjoyed making some doll clothes and doing a few pictures using my nice water color box. It is all rite as long as I am good at my lessons. Now it's getting toward Christmas. Can you believe it? I could not until a present came from dear Mr. Roosevelt and little Eleanor. It came all the way from Europe and Mama says my little friend is now in Europe with her dear parents. Isn't that wonderful, Diary?

Sorrento, Italy
Nov. 23, '90

My dear Elsie,

Your little friend Eleanor Roosevelt whom I hope you remember for she talks always so much of you and thinks of your wonderfully done Prince and the Pauper this Christmas and wishes her father to send you from her the little gift with this. She bought it herself and would like to write to you herself but she is not yet old enough.

Give my kindest regards to your mother and father and do not forget how much we all enjoyed your acting and what a great future you have before you.

Your affectionate friend,
Elliott Roosevelt

P.S. I wish I could tell you of the wonderful Bay of Naples and the great burning volcano Vesuvious; it would be more interesting than Doll's stories but it is late and you are probably tired. A Merry Christmas and a Happy New Year from Eleanor and me.

Well, Eleanor isn't as old as me but we have been friends for a long time and I love her verry much. The little picture is of her. I think the nicest thing about Christmas is hearing from old friends, don't you?

Christmas is over and Mr. Frohman has decided we will go south where no-one has seen the Prince and the Pauper yet. Mama is pleased. Dora doesn't want to go but she will.

Hartford,
Thursday

Dear Elsie,

I wonder if you and your parents and Dora are really at Poultney now. Mr. Gillette says you were going there. I want to be sure you are there because I have a set of books that I want to send you with my warm love. They may be a little old for you now but I think there are parts you will enjoy but later you will enjoy more.

Would you like me to send them to Poultney or is there any other place that you would rather have them sent?

I did not send them to Boston or Chicago because I was afraid while you were away they might bother you.

Will you please write and tell me as soon as you receive this where to send them.

We leave here now in a few days and I want to send them before we go away.

I hope you and your mother and Dora are well. How I wish you could come in and play with Jean — it is a rainy afternoon and I think you could have a good time together in the house particularly if you could bring Todkins, too.

Please give my regards to your parents,

With love to you and Dora, believe me,

Always affectionately yours,
Olivia L. Clemens.

Dora wants to answer this kind letter and says I can write to Mrs. Clemens after the books arrive. That they are coming makes me think of how many children there are in the world who haven't even one book, and I have books upon books. So I ought to be the happiest little girl on earth. I think I am.

Oh, it IS good to be home again at darling Road's End. How verry much I do love it! Elsa Carroll who is my best friend is coming to stay for a whole week. I am angshus to hear all about her school and her trip to Paris, France. I want to go there VERRY much but first I want to go to school with Elsa at Miss Ely's Classes for Young Ladies. And Mama has promised me I shall after we finish touring The Prince and the Pauper. Oh. I forgot. Miss Ely visited us for the weekend to talk about my education with Mama. Miss Elizabeth Ely runs this school with her two sisters and her brother who is Mr. Arthur Ely. Elsa says Miss Elizabeth is the most important and I think she is just loverly. She is verry understanding and I think I shall love her verry much the way I do Mrs. Dodge. Miss Ely and I had several good talks and she said if I work regularly with a good teacher while I am away I will soon catch up. She thought that I could go in the class with Elsa Carroll and Hazel Hatch. Miss Ely was pleased with my French and this made me verry happy. She said if I went on as I have begun I should improve enough to go in the French class with Lavinia Avery. I was thrilled as Elsa says Lavinia is the smartest girl in the whole school. . . . Oh, dear, dear, will I ever get there? Do you know something, Diary dear? Elsa says she envies me being in the theater and seeing so much of the world even if I haven't been to Paris. And sometimes I envy HER. Well — that seems to be the way things are. Oh!! Another thing. Miss Ely has arranged for a friend of hers who gave Lavinia Avery special lessons to be my new Governess. She will go on tour with us which will be fine as Miss Ely says she is wonderful. She is Mlle. Jeanne Racinet and is from Paris, too!

The days fly by I'm sorry to say. I do so love the times here at our darling little cottage with its dear little name "Road's End" which I thot of myself. I can lie in my bed and look at the Green Mountains beyond Lake St. Catherine which is at the bottom of our land and I can hear the waves from the lake when the wind blows them to the shore. Papa has fixed the hammock in the little wood beyond the old well and that is where I take my nap in the afternoon while Mama is sewing or nodding in her chair. Yes, Dearest Diary, it is so loverly to come back to all this after another time away — such a long time, too, when I neglected you. Would lots of kisses help make up for it? Here they are. XXXXXX The season wasn't too hard and Mama and Mr. Frohman are encouraged to see how well The Prince and the P. went outside New York City. So we can enjoy what Papa calls a "breather" here at Poultney all the more. I'm so happy I don't know where to begin.

I think I'll tell you about the dear cows even if it is rather a sad story. A poor cow was killed on the railroad tracks yesterday. Something was the matter with the cow-catcher which didn't work rite when the poor things strayed across the tracks and one poor little calf was run over. I spoke to Mr. Johnson the station master about it and he said it was mighty bad but that such things do happen but I said I thot the driver should stop the train and help the animals to safety but Mr. Johnson said there was not time for this and trains had to have a cow-catcher or the trains would get off the track and people would be killed. He thot the trouble this time was becoz this cow-catcher was broken. He said the engineer was a nice man who was verry sad about the calf and he had reported the trouble to head-quarters so I said I would write to my friend Mr. Chauncey Depew who is the President of the Railroad. I would ask him to speak to the drivers on the line and ask them to be extra careful and also see that the train inspectors attend to all cow catchers to be sure they worked rite.

Mama and Dora who was here for a few days smiled about this but Papa said I was doing a good thing and he thot I was his good girl. I worked hard on my letter to Mr. Depew and I wrote it several times before Papa corrected it and addressed the envelope. He took it into the Post Office himself when he and Mama were out driving. I hope I get an answer soon. It has all been very worrying.

Indeed I was so angshus I talked to Leo about it as soon as he came and he said I needn't worry any more about the poor cows. He will speak to Mr. Depew about it and I'm sure he will becoz as I have told you many times he never says he will do something unless he does it right off. Yes, he is my dearest trustable friend and I love him more all the time.

Well, here is the letter from Mr. Depew. Leo said he was a very prompt man and he was!

NEW YORK CENTRAL HUDSON RIVER RAILROAD CO.

GRAND CENTRAL DEPOT

CHAUNCEY DEPEW, PRESIDENT.

New York   July 11, 1891.

Dear Miss Elsie,

I have your letter of July 2nd. The road of which you speak I have nothing whatever to do with. I am not an officer of it, nor a director, nor a stock-holder. Poultney is on The Delaware Hudson Canal Company's road. The President of that road is Mr. R. M. Olyphant, and his office is at 21 Courtland Street, New York. I am sure if you will write him as nice a letter as you have written me that Valhalla Glen will be safer than it is now.

Your very truly,
Chauncey M. Depew.

Miss Elsie Leslie Lyde.

Leo thot Mr. Depew's letter was VERRY amusing and he esplaned to me about this preshus place being called Valhalla Glen and he gave me a kiss becoz he is sure this story will have a happy ending. I like stories that come out well. I suppose that's why I was at one time so crazy about the Alger books, spechuly the "Dandy Dick" stories. I wrote to Mr. Alger and told him so and he sent me all his books with my name inside from my friend Horatio Alger, Jr. They are all on the shelves in my play house. Mama and Mlle. do not approve of them but I shall keep them anyway becoz of Mr. Alger's kind thots. Also, I don't think they are so bad. Here is a letter to keep, dear Diary. It's from Mr. Alger.

Robert Morrison Olyphant (1824–1917), railroad magnate.

249 West 34th St.
New York
April 24, 1890

My dear little friend Elsie,

I am pleased to receive your letter, which reached me late last evening after my return from Otto Hegner's farewell concert. It was very successful, and he received quite an ovation — This morning he sailed for Europe. He may come back next year, but in the mean time he has promised to write to me — He sent a letter from Chicago early this month, in which he wrote me that he thought of beccomming a cow-boy! I shall give you credit for your Chicago letter — I am sorry it did not reach me — still if it had come to me after its contact with the ice-pitcher I might have been surprised at Elsie's sending me such a cold letter —

I am sure you will enjoy your visit to San Francisco — The people there are warm-hearted and cordial, and I think you will have a warm reception — Shall you stop on the way?

I am glad you enjoyed the book I sent you — If Mr. Pearson will send me a list of the books you already have, I shall know what to send you next time —

Please remember me kindly to your mother and sister, and accept much love for your-self —

Your sincere friend
Horatio Alger, Jr.

William Faversham

Everything, dear Diary, is now all excitement becoz we are going out West with The Prince and the Pauper, Mr. William Faversham is grand as Miles Hendon, and Mama

---

Otto Hegner, a pianist of genius, was a child prodigy. His career was sadly cut short by an early death.

<table>
<tr><td colspan="4">

Daniel Frohman's Prince and Pauper Co.

R O U T E .

</td></tr>
</table>

JULY	28.	One Week	....Denver, Col.
AUG.	4.		....Colorado Springs, "
"	5.		....Pueblo, "
"	6.	TRAVEL.	
"	7. }		....Salt Lake City, Utah
"	8. }		
"	9. }		....San Francisco, Cal.
"	11.	Two Weeks	
"	25.		....San Diego, "
"	26.		....San Bernardino, "
"	27. }		
"	28. }		....Los Angelos, "
"	29. }		
"	30. }		
SEPT.	1. }		....Oakland, "
"	2. }		....San Jose, "
"	3.		....Stockton, "
"	4.		....Sacremento, "
"	5. }		
"	6 }		....Portland, Oregon
"	8.	One Week	
"	15.		....Seattle, W. T.
"	16. }		....Tacoma, "
"	17. }		
"	18. }	TRAVEL.	
"	19. }		
"	20. }		
"	22. }		....Omaha, Neb.
"	23 }		
"	24. }		....Sioux City, "
"	26. }		
"	27. }		....Council Bluffs, Iowa
"	29.		~~Des Moines~~, "
"	30.		....Cedar Rapids, "
OCT.	1.		....Dubuque, "
"	2.		....Davenport, "
"	3.		....Bloomington, Ill.
"	4.		....Peoria, "
"	6. }		....Springfield, "
"	7. }		....Terre Haute, Ind.
"	8.		
"	9.		....Columbus, Ohio
"	10. }		
"	11. }		

is so pleased that he has agreed to go on the tour. I loved acting with him these past months. He is verry handsome I think even more so than dear Mr. Vanderfelt or Mr. Elliott. But I love them all. Poor Papa cannot go with us. Dr. Clough says he must not so he will return to his old home town of Newark and stay with the Winans. They are his favorite relatives and will take good care of him. I hope he will not get too lonesome for us. What a great thing dear Mr. Frohman is doing for Mama. She says people will think it is HIS tour but Mama is really doing it. She thinks we will make enough money to pay for my education and take us all to Europe, Papa too if he is well and wants to come along. I hope so but sometimes I'm afraid Papa will never get well and strong. But Dr. Clough says he will if he gets enough rest and good food and fresh air. I spose these hard trips and queer hours would not be good for him spechully when he gets a bad spell of asma. I think Papa is wonderful the way he never lets on how he feels about things. I realy think he understands how crazy Mama and Dora are about the theater and he always sends us off with a smile.

Now, dear Diary, you will want to know where we are going with the play. Here is the schedule.

What going about, dear Diary! It is now another year — 1892. And we are again on tour with The Prince and the Pauper. While at Toledo I had a little more time so I decided to finish my poem of The Prince and the Pauper at which I worked verry hard. When I had finished it I decided to write to Mr. Oliver Wendell Holmes who was so kind to me in Boston and ask him what he thot of it. Dear Mr. Holmes liked both Fauntleroy and this play so I think he will help me. Mama did not want me to do this at first but later when I had asked her again she looked over my letter and said I could send it. This is what I wrote —

Oliver Wendell Holmes

My dear Mr. Holmes,

I hope you will not think I am a very tiresome little girl for bothering you so soon but this is a very serious question. Will you tell me what you think of the rhymes I send you with my letter. This is the longest rhyme I have ever written. I love to write but no one ever tells me what they really think when they read them they just smile. But you know so much you know just what I want to say and cannot.

I don't want to tire you but do you think them verry bad? I have heard you love little children and perhaps you will love me and write me what you think. You were so kind and wrote me such a lovely letter. I am verry proud to have it and it is among my choicest treasures. The rhyme is taken from the drama by Mrs. Abby Sage Richardson but the story as you know is written by my loyal friend Mark Twain in all his letters to me he always signs himself so and is verry loyal. I do not know much about where to put the commas and periods and you must not think I can spell all the large words I write for I cannot. I am not as clever as most little girls of eleven years old. When I am writing and cannot spell the words I ask someone and they tell me. I had to have it type-written for my first copy was so mixed up no one could read it but myself and I had to read it to the typewriter.

Your devoted little friend,
Elsie Leslie.

After trying not to watch for the Postman, dear Diary, I was finally rewarded when this letter came from dear Mr. Holmes.

BOODY HOUSE,

WELCH & HARDY,
PROPRIETORS.

Toledo, O. March 6 1892

My dear Mr Holmes

I hope you will not think I am a very tiresome little girl for bothering you again so soon, but this is a very serious question. Will you tell me what you think of the rhymes I send you with my letter. This is the longest rhyme I have ever written. I love to write but no one ever tells me what they really think when they read them they just smile. But you know oh so much you know just what I want to say and can not. I dont want to tire you but do you think them very bad I have heard you love little children and perhaps will love me and write me what you

of eleven years and a half old When I am writing and

BOODY HOUSE,

189

and letter it choisest is taken a by you know friend his letter himself ol I do t when l periods ink I e words am not girls

BOODY HOUSE,

WELCH & HARDY,
PROPRIETORS.

Toledo, O. 189

the word I ask they tell me it typewritten copy was so one could read I had to read it tter

devoted ind ie Leslie Lyde

196 Beacon Street
Boston, Mass.
March 10th 1892

My Dear Little Girl,

I have read your poem all through carefully, and I have read about you in the Magazines and looked at the charming pictures which show you as Elsie and as Little Lord Fauntleroy. Of course I have been interested in all this reading. But you won't like me when I tell you what I think of your poetry. I am afraid you will be disappointed when I give you my opinion, for I have observed that we poets as poets are very sensitive about our productions. A great while ago a Roman writer spoke about what he called "genus irritabile natum" — the irritable race of poets.

I think you are in too much of a hurry. You are not ripe for verse as yet, whatever may be your natural gifts. You do not even spell correctly, as you confess. You do not construct your lines accurately — some are too long, some too short. You do not seem to know true rhymes from imperfect jingles — for instance

Here are	beating	
	weaping	
a few	king	beguiled
	seen	I vile
specimens		
	in	mistress
of	bring	best
your false rhymes	him	descend
	in	men
which are really no		
rhymes at all.	arm	him	met
	barn	2. in	felt.

I should advise you to wait until you have studied good verse a few years before attempting to write poetry. Your prose is better and if you write at all you had better stick to that. But why do you want to write at your age? I think you would do much better to study. Leave the green fruit on the bough. It may ripen if you give it time, until it becomes sweet and mellow.

However, if you feel that you MUST write I strongly advise you to keep to prose for the present.

I am afraid you are sorry you asked for my advice, but I have given you my honest opinion, and you had better reflect upon it and see if it is not worth following.

I am, my dear little Elsie,

Most sincerely yours,
Oliver Wendell Holmes.

What a wise and wonderful letter, isn't it, Dear Diary? Mr. Holmes is right of course. And so are Miss Ely and my dear Mlle. Racinet who both say when I am twelve I must begin the study of Latin. They told me sometime ago that I must learn Latin if I wish to write well. I will now ask Mlle. to get after my bad spelling . . . so pull up, Elsie, and work harder at your lessons.

Dear Old Diary (as Mr. Sothern would say)

It is now 1893. Can you believe it? We are now back in dear old New York and it's December AND all those tours of my darling Play are over!! AND after the holidays I will start to SCHOOL. About time, too, as my dear Mlle. remarked the other day, "Quite time unless I expect to go through life spelling VERY with 2 R's." She also spoke about LOVERLY saying it needed no R. at all. I was VERY polite and said, "Of course, dear Mlle." But I felt very two faced because in my heart I like loveRly much better.

Our new place up town is very nice and not too far from the school. Elsa will be my desk mate which is very nice of dear Miss Ely. Elsa says I will not like getting up early but I shall have to as school takes in at half past nine! I am indeed VERY happy with so much to look forward to as Mr. Irving and Miss Terry are here from London in their wonderful plays at the new Abby Theater. I sent Mr. Irving one of my poems to welcome them and asked him if I could have two tickets for Mama and me (or Dora) to see one of the plays. Dora took my letter around to the Plaza Hotel where he is staying.

My dear Diary,

Before we came back home to New York we were in Philadelphia for two weeks. One day it was VERY exciting because I invited all the little newsboys to the matinee and they all came. Mr. Frohman came over for it and he had special tickets printed for them. The tickets said:

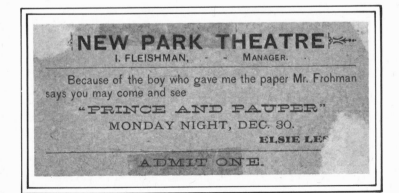

NEW PARK THEATRE
I. FLEISHMAN, - - MANAGER.
Because of the boy who gave me the paper Mr. Frohman says you may come and see
"PRINCE AND PAUPER"
MONDAY NIGHT, DEC. 30.
ELSIE LE
ADMIT ONE.

The house was full of children and they all enjoyed it. The little newsboys clapped and shouted and when things got verry bad for Prince Edward, they called out, "Don't youse hurt the kid—" and "Dat's right, Milsey, Bully fer you." The grown ups there said, "Hush-hush" to them but they went right on they were so excited. I didn't mind because I felt it was so verry real to them. At the end they wanted me to make a speech but I ran away and hid until the Prompter found me and I had to go in front of the curtain and bow and take a basket of flowers. The letter on it said:

Dere Miss Elsie, won't you please to send the baskit back to the store wot lent it to us? We cud only raise enuf money fer der flowers but we wanted yer to have em becoz we think youre jist swell. yours truly,
The Newsboys of Philadelphia

Did you EVER? . . . Yes, I took the basket back to the flower shop and the man was verry pleased and shook hands with me and gave me a bunch of violets. Mama said she hoped the poor little fellows didn't go without their supper to pay for those flowers and so do I. That would be just AWFUL. Dear Mr. Frohman said I needn't worry about that. Do you suppose he helped them pay for it?

Newsboys in Elsie Leslie's time were not unionized. However, such public spirited men as President Theodore Roosevelt and Horatio Alger, Jr. were among their many benefactors. The first Newsboys Home in New York, founded by Charles Loring Brace (1826–1890), was in the loft of the old Sun building in lower Manhattan.

Here is a letter from Mr. Irving which came this morning.

Plaza Hotel

My dear Little Friend,

   Come on Friday — it will be a pleasure to welcome you.

                     With all good wishes,
                     Sincerely yours,
                     Henry Irving.

Miss Elsie Leslie

D**earest, dearest** D**iary,**

It was so wonderful to see Mr. Irving but Miss Terry was not there. Yes, Mama and I went as he said on Friday. He was so kind. He had the tickets for "Becket" in his pocket and also, he gave us a lovely tea. He said he thought I would like "Becket" more than the other plays as there is a little Prince in it. The part is played by a little boy. His name is Leo Byrne. Mr. Irving did not say how old he is, just that he is a nice child and Mr. Irving thought it was too bad that he didn't have many children to play with. I wonder if his parents are in the company but I didn't like to ask. I also wondered if his hair is curly or if he wears a wig like Tommy did when he was Fauntleroy. From what Dora tells me about "Becket" I think it must be a verry sad play. She says I will not understand all of it but that I will love the poetry and the beautiful dresses. I wish I could see all the plays. There are two more, "The Merchant of Venice" and "The Bells." I wish particlaly to see "The Merchant of Venice" which I have read and which is my idea of a real Fairy Tale. AND I want to play Portia some-

day. But Mama says one play is enough just now. I was verry downcast until dear Mrs. Carroll came and said she wanted to take me to this with Elsa for my Christmas present. Mama said I could go so I am indeed verry happy that another wish has been granted.

Here it is the night before Christmas '93 and verry warm — Papa says too warm to snow but maybe he is mistaken. It would be nice to have snow for Christmas, wouldn't it, dear Diary?

   It's Christmas Day and no snow and no sleighbells but the poor Postman, still working, came with a lot of letters. On top of the others there was a very special letter for me from Hartford. I opened it very carefully and read it aloud to Papa, Mama, and Dora and they laughed and laughed. Here it is! It is the most preshus of all my presents.

The Players
Christmas, '93

Hello! is it you, Elsie?

   I wish you lived in this state. I would go straight to see you. But 103rd Street! If I had only known it — for I was right there in the neighborhood yesterday — out there by Chicago.
   Lord, I do hate travel and do hate to get lost, too — but the minute I get hands on your Uncle Gillette! I will re-quire him to take me to 103rd Street — and he shall do it, too, or I will tie his legs around his neck and throw him out of the window.
   With love to you and Miss Dora & kindest regards to your mother,

                     I am yours to command,
                     S. L. Clemens

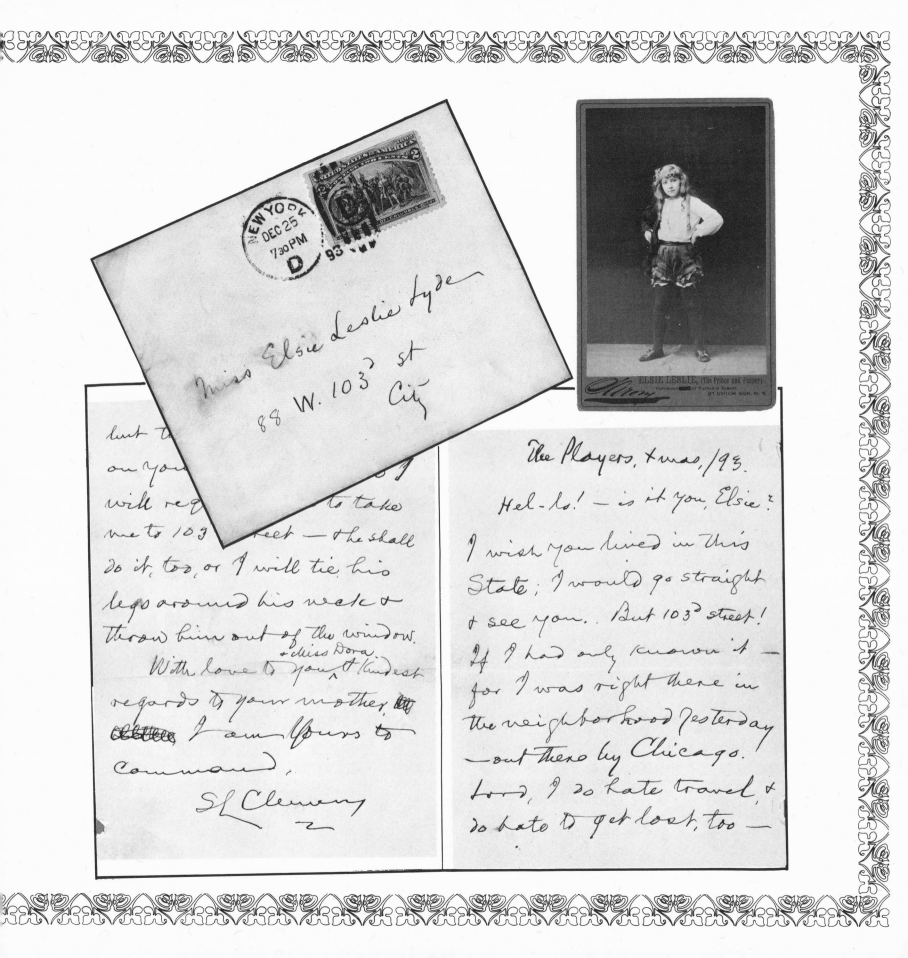

Envelope:

NEW YORK
DEC 25
7:30 PM
D

Miss Elsie Leslie Lyde
88 W. 103ᵈ St
City

Photograph caption:

ELSIE LESLIE, (The Prince and Pauper)
87 UNION SQR. N.Y.

Letter, right page:

The Players, Xmas, /93.

Hel-lo! — is it you, Elsie?
I wish you lived in this
State; I would go straight
+ see you. But 103ᵈ street!
If I had only known it —
for I was right there in
the neighborhood Yesterday
— out there by Chicago.
Lord, I so hate travel, +
so hate to get lost, too —

Letter, left page:

but t...
on you...
will re... to take
me to 103... Street — + he shall
do it, too, or I will tie his
legs around his neck +
throw him out of the window.
        With love to you + Miss Dora. + kindest
regards to your mother, ~~...~~
~~...~~ I am Yours to
Command,
            SL Clemens

This is the first day of 1894. Last night Mama let me stay up as late as Dora did. It made me feel verry grown up, dear Diary.

January 4, 1894

$\mathcal{G}$ood morning, $\mathcal{D}$iary,

Guess what? I am really going to school — to Miss Ely's! So I'll be with Elsa and Hazel at last, and maybe I'll learn to spell. It will seem strange to stay in one place and get up every morning at the same time. I think I will like it. I can hardly wait for tomorrow.

January 5th

Well, I DID like it. Miss Ely took me aside and said, "Well, Elsie, dear, here you are at last, I feel sure you will enjoy the girls and make a place for yourself in the school just as you have in a world they know little about. Remember we are all glad to have you here and we all want you to be happy. From what I know of you, I think you will be." Wasn't that WONDERFUL?

"And, indeed, I was happy at Miss Ely's," Elsie said many years after those halcyon days had become favorite memories. "Yes, they were the best times, I think. I managed very well as I had the highest marks in my class. For graduation there were lots of presents, too. One of the most precious was a picture from my dear Mr. Hutton, which he sent, characteristically, some time after the actual day. With his photograph — and I'm glad it is a good one — he wrote these lines, which even now, cause much merriment.

A Little Lord, a Little King:
A Little Pauper — Prince, beside:
A Little Queen in Every thing:
A Little Elsie Leslie Lyde.

A Little King, a Little Lord:
A Prince and Burglar, side by side:
We'd feel that TRUTH was all abroad:
If Little Elsie Leslie Lied!

Onteora. July 4th 1896 —

Laurence Hutton

Elsie (right) and her sister Dora, c. 1896

"Best of all, Mama was entirely pleased with all the time and expense of my years at Miss Ely's wonderful school. This made me so happy and I was even happier with Mama's graduation gift which was the trip to Europe. In June she, Dora and I sailed from New York for Southampton on the SS. *St. Louis*. It was a gay crossing, especially for Dora who was very popular with the Yale boys who were over to compete in the Henley Boat Races.

"Some weeks later," continued Elsie, taking from the table beside her a worn little volume — one of her diaries — "I wrote this from the Hotel Metropole, London — yes, it was July 7, 1896."

Dearest Diary,

You will be as excited as I am about this. This morning I was in the Writing Room starting a letter to Papa when I was interrupted by that handsome young man, Hr. Harry Sillcoks. He was all dressed up ready to go to the Henley Races, in white ducks with his field glasses over his shoulder, and carrying his little kodak, too. He said, "How strange things come about in this life, don't they Elsie? When I used to see you act, I never thought we should be in London at the same time and I should be asking you to come with me to The Regatta. Will you?" — Well, I was too surprised to say anything but, "Oh, I'd LOVE to but we must ask Mama, which he did and OF COURSE she said I was too young, but she'd be delighted to have him take Dora." The poor fellow was very upset but so well behaved, what could he do but agree? so Dora went and I think it was unfair, don't you, Diary? She has so many Beaux after her, especially a gentleman we met on the ship. He's much older than Dora is but he's very good looking. Also, he's VERRY rich, which as Mama says is not a bad thing. Oh, dear, dear, I AM put out. Just think of dear old Yale going to the race and me not there to see it! Oh, well, Pull up, Elsie!

"I often had to tell myself to 'Pull Up,'" said Elsie with a smile as she put the little book away.

Epilogue

At the end of the summer of 1896, which was the year of the first trip to Europe, after a time in Scotland and England, Mama took Elsie to Paris where she placed her under the guidance of the beloved French governess, who had returned home to live. Satisfied with this arrangement, Mama rejoined Dora and they returned to America.

Nearly two years went by. Then, in late September, 1898 came the golden opportunity for Elsie to return to the stage. This was Joe Jefferson's offer for her to play Lydia Languish in his proposed all-star revival of *The Rivals*, the delightful Restoration comedy by Sheridan.

Richard Brinsley Sheridan (1751–1816), famous Restoration playwright, born in Dublin and educated at Oxford. Mr. Sheridan followed David Garrick as the manager of the Drury Lane Theatre. He was the author of *The Rivals, The School for Scandal,* and *The Critic*.

FIFTH AVENUE THEATRE

Broadway and Twenty-Eighth Street.   Sole Manager.

EDWIN KNOWLES,

Commencing Monday Evening, Oct. 10, 1898.

Evenings at 8.15.   Matinee Saturday at 2 30.

CARRIAGE PARTIES WILL BE RECEIVED AT 28th ST. ENTRANCE.

ENGAGEMENT OF

JOSEPH JEFFERSON

COMEDY CO.,

presenting Richard Brinsley Sheridan's Three Act Comedy,

THE

RIVALS.

CAST.

	Verner Clarges
Sir Antony Absolute	Otis Skinner
Captain Absolute, under the assumed name of Beverly	Wilton Lackaye
	JOSEPH JEFFERSON
Sir Lucius O'Trigger	Joseph Warren
Bob Acres	Geo. Denham
Faulkland	Walter B. Woodall
David	Ffolliett Paget
Fag	Elsie Leslie
Mrs. Malaprop	Blanche Bender
Lydia	
Lucy	

Programme Continued on Second Page Following.

CALIFORNIA.
Special Vestibuled Trains, consisting of sleeping, dining, library and observation cars, will leave the eastern cities frequently for California, Mexico, etc. Information and circulars about these or other trips can be had on application.

RAYMOND & WHITCOMB,
TOURS AND TICKETS,
31 EAST 14TH STREET, UNION SQUARE WEST, NEW YORK.

FIFTH AVE THEATRE
Broadway and 28th
MR. EDWIN KNOWLES, SOLE MANAGER

THE LEO VON RAVEN PUBLISHING CO
113 E. 14TH ST.
NEW YORK.

Joseph Jefferson as Bob Acres in *The Rivals*

Otis Skinner as Jack Absolute in *The Rivals*

Fortunately for Elsie, Mrs. Carroll and Elsa were winding up a summer in Europe and they arrived in Paris in time for the two chums to have a gay time together in that lovelist of cities before the three sailed for New York. Somewhat to Elsie's embarrassment, dear Mrs. Carroll could not refrain from saying to willing listeners how proud she was to be taking Elsie home to star in a forthcoming production by Joe Jefferson. Indeed, explained Mrs. Carroll, Elsie Leslie would be the youngest actress ever to play Lydia Languish with him. This was not the foremost thought in Elsie's mind, as thrilled as she was about it. She could only dream of the joy of working once more with her wonderful old friend.

The eagerly anticipated revival of *The Rivals,* as arranged by Mr. Jefferson in three acts rather than the usual lengthy five, opened in New York at the fashionable Fifth Avenue Theatre on the evening of October 10th, 1898. In it Joe Jefferson was once more to delight everyone fortunate enough to see him as Bob Acres, and Jack Absolute was none other than Otis Skinner.

The morning after, too stimulated to sleep, Elsie Leslie wrote and put in the programme of the play this account of the performance:

"It was really too wonderful last night! All the people in the cast were superb, and oh, so very kind to me! Also, Mama tells me that Mr. Jefferson says that he considers this his best production of *The Rivals*. My cup of joy is full what with that and so many telegrams, letters and beautiful flowers. Dear Mr. Birch wrote me the sweetest poem on a darling picture and sent it in a big box of American Beauty roses. Oh! I DO hope he can afford it. And before I left for the theatre about seven o'clock a messenger boy came bringing me a present from dear Mr. Jefferson. It's a cut glass cookie jar with a lovely silver top which says —

E.L.L.
SOUVENIR
October, 10th 1898

And it's full of cookies, too. There is nobody like him in all the world!"

To Elsie Leslie, it was the greatest and happiest milestone and she was often to say that Joe Jefferson was sometimes labelled as the delineator of but one part. His reply to this was, "It is certainly better to play one part and make it various than to play many parts and make them all alike." It is true that Rip Van Winkle was Mr. Jefferson's greatest role. It is also true that his portrayal of Rip is considered one of the most brilliant and beautiful creations of the stage. Indeed, many believe, as did Elsie Leslie, that beyond the range of Shakespearean plays, none has so captured the heart of America as *Rip Van Winkle*. Had he done nothing else, and he did a great deal more, Joe Jefferson was certainly America's best loved actor and his influence upon his profession will never be erased.

The Tiffany cookie jar, its sterling silver top still undimmed, and the charming photographs of Elsie Leslie as Lydia Languish (and it is by no means an easy role, often overplayed) are treasured mementoes of this notable revival of the famous play. Youthful, as indeed Lydia Languish must be, graceful and thoughtful, Elsie Leslie's interpretation of the part revealed that she was, at heart, the same "trustable child" who loved to receive these letters from her "preshus" friends and kept them so carefully. It may have been this quality that made her so enchanting a Lydia Languish. Her delicate beauty and the naturalness of her playing enabled Elsie Leslie to hold her own with the artists Mr. Jefferson had engaged for this, his last, and in his estimation, his best production of *The Rivals*. She was just eighteen.

Elsie Leslie as
Lydia Languish
in *The Rivals*